A Treasury of Jewels and Gems

A TREASURY of JEWELS and GEMS

MONA CURRAN

NEW YORK

EMERSON BOOKS INC.

NK
7304
.C8
1962

© MONA CURRAN 1961, 1962
LIBRARY OF CONGRESS CATALOG NUMBER: 62-14812
ALL RIGHTS RESERVED
MANUFACTURED IN THE UNITED STATES OF AMERICA

For Hugh, with love

Acknowledgements

The author gratefully acknowledges the generous help given her by expert gemmologists and jewellers, particularly with the scientific details.

For the section on Diamonds much is owed to De Beers Consolidated Mines Company and their experts.

Grateful acknowledgement is also made to Mr George D. Skinner of N. W. Ayer & Son Inc. of New York City, and to Miss Dorothy Dignam, the well-known writer and authority on diamonds, who provided many of the American details in the chapter on Regency and Victorian Jewellery, as well as the delightful American illustrations.

Contents

1	The five precious gems	11
2	Some gemstones	30
3	Rings	41
4	The bracelet	47
5	The necklace	53
6	The ear-ring	61
7	Brooches and clips	66
8	Tiaras and hair ornaments	73
9	Regency and Victorian jewellery	78
10	Some royal jewels	92
11	The Crown Jewels of England	106
12	Birthstones	114
13	Setting and cutting gems	121
14	Some famous gems and their history	127
15	On choosing jewels	140
16	Caring for your jewels	144
17	'Jewel' anniversaries	148
Index		149

CHAPTER ONE

The five precious gems

I. Diamonds

Truly and appropriately has the diamond been described as the King of Gems for surely it is the very monarch of all precious stones, desired by women in all walks of life and of every age.

That it remains for ever the paramount choice for an engagement ring; that it gives grandeur to all royal occasions; that it for ever holds its beauty are facts which are incontestable. What makes this the most appealing and valuable of all gems is, perhaps, its unexampled fire, brilliance and magnificence and its unfailing fascination.

Centuries before the Christian era diamonds were treasured by the ancient Hindus and many of their finest stones were used to decorate the temples or were set into the brows of their idols. Some of the most famous diamonds in the world today were once the prized gems of these ancient civilizations.

The story of the diamond began more than a thousand million years ago—millions of years before man appeared on the earth. The centre of the earth was its birthplace, where the raging furnaces and terrific pressures set up underneath the earth's cooling crust turned an insignificant lump of carbon into the clear, brilliant diamond. Thus Nature produced her masterpiece of the mineral world, the most precious, the most useful and most beautiful of all the jewels.

Although records of past civilizations indicate that diamonds were known more than 3,000 years before Christ, there is no record of the finding of the first diamond. India seems to have been the first source of diamonds: was, in fact, the treasure house of the ancient world. From that vast territory came not only the peerless diamond, but precious metals and gems of every hue. Golconda—a name which even today conjures up visions of fabulous wealth—was the jewel centre of the world. Right up to the early eighteenth century India maintained her supremacy as the diamond centre of the world, but the seventeenth and eighteenth centuries were times of great adventure and it was in 1725 that a band of Portuguese adventurers landing in South America led to the dramatic discovery of diamonds in Brazil. For the next 150 years Brazil dominated the world's diamond markets, substantially increasing the wealth of Portugal in particular. But the South African fields, greatest source of diamonds in the world, had yet to be discovered. When that happened, it was accidental.

In the 1860's a travelling trader named O'Reilly outspanned his oxen at the farm of a friend. Lying on the table in the kitchen were several pebbles picked up from the banks of the Vaal river by the farmer's children. One of these pebbles attracted O'Reilly and he offered to buy it. The friend's wife, however, protesting that it was only a child's toy, insisted O'Reilly should accept it as a gift. This 'child's toy' was the first South African diamond and was later sold for £500.

From this simple beginning have sprung up the great diamond mines of Kimberley (the 'Big Hole'), De Beers Mine, Dutoitspan, Premier and Jagersfontein, to mention but a few of the famous ones. The South African and Tanganyikan diamond fields are interesting in that the diamonds are found embedded in soft blue rock, known as blue-ground, running in underground pipes or veins, frequently at a great depth. Mine shafts have to be sunk to reach them and bring the diamond-bearing clay to the surface, where it is crushed and washed and sifted to extract the stones. In other parts of the world diamonds are found very much nearer the surface, sometimes actually on the surface of the ground. These near-the-surface sites are called 'alluvial' deposits. Alluvial deposits originated as a result of the erosion of the earth's surface by rain, sun and wind which released many of the diamonds from the surrounding rock and carried them down the river beds to their present positions. The diamond fields of India and Brazil were alluvial and so are the diamond areas of west Southwest Africa, the Congo Republic and Angola. But whatever the source of diamonds, from deep-mining or from alluvial deposits, their extraction is a long and arduous process, calling for skill, endurance and patience.

To the layman, the word 'diamond' conjures up a picture of a sparkling gem. Such is the finished jewel, but the rough diamond looks rather like a lump of washing soda and very few people would recognize it as a diamond. In this rough state diamonds are sorted and graded by the experts who decide which are suitable for gemstones and which shall be used for industrial purposes. Only about one-quarter of all diamonds mined are suitable for gem purposes.

London, England, is the Golconda of the modern mining industry. To London come over eighty per cent of the world's diamonds. To London also come diamond buyers from all over the world, eager to see what stones will be offered at the diamond 'sights' as they are called. In the course of their regular visits to the 'sights' accredited buyers become known and where strangers are naturally closely scrutinized the accredited buyers are admitted without question to the inner sanctum of the 'sights'. In the course of time buyers become well acquainted with the selling assortment and some may even seldom examine the whole 'parcel' of their allocation; though they may, of course, if they wish, examine each individual diamond, even the small mêlée. The prospective purchaser usually studies a 'parcel' for a few minutes, and during that time he will decide whether or not to buy—the transaction is as simple as that.

The fate of the diamond after it has left the diamond 'sights' depends on its quality; only a small proportion are used for gems.

With fine diamonds, destined to become fine jewels, the expert examines the rough diamond crystal and decides how the diamond shall be cleft or sawn—the first stages in producing the faceted gem. This operation is a very highly skilled one and requires a thorough understanding of crystal structure.

Until comparatively recent years cleaving was the only method adopted for dividing a diamond. The introduction of sawing represents the only advance in the technique of diamond cutting for many years. The cleavage plane would be determined and a tiny scratch made on the rough stone with a diamond-pointed tool at the point where the cleaver was to deliver his hammer tap. One sharp blow at this point and the diamond would divide cleanly into two along its 'cleavage plane'. This apparently simple process calls for the very highest skill, for an error in determining the cleavage point or in the angle at which the blow is struck might mean that a valuable diamond is ruined. Instead of splitting into two with clean, smooth edges, the diamond might shatter into fragments or be split into jagged-edged pieces.

When a highly important diamond is concerned the responsibility is overwhelming. The cutter entrusted with the cleaving of the great Cullinan diamond—that world-famous gem—was so overcome by the magnitude of his task and responsibility that when he had successfully made his 'strike' he collapsed and had to receive medical attention.

Today the sawing method—particularly in the case of smaller stones—is the more popular. The advantage of sawing over cleaving for small- or medium-sized stones is that two equal-sized brilliants can be cut from one crystal, whereas with cleaving only one brilliant and a few smaller fragments are produced from the crystal.

For sawing, fragile little discs of phosphor bronze, about three inches in diameter and less than one-tenth of a millimetre in thickness, are used. It is fascinating to watch a battery of these tiny saws revolving at a tremendous speed apparently cutting with perfect ease into the diamond, following the thick line of black ink marked on the stone by the expert who determines the plane along which the diamond is to be sawn. Though seemingly a thin disc of metal is doing the work of cutting the hardest known substance—a diamond—the secret lies in the fine diamond dust, bound in oil, with which the saws are lubricated, the diamond dust actually doing the cutting. It takes about a day to cut through a diamond of one carat.

After the stones have been divided by sawing or cleaving they are 'bruted' to give them their first rough shape as gems. 'Bruting' is a sort of chipping method. One diamond, cemented into a holder, is rotated in a fast-spinning machine. Another diamond, cemented into a similar holder, is held firmly against the revolving diamond by a skilled operator, and as small fragments of diamond are chipped off the gem gradually takes on its first rough shape. These little chips or fragments are carefully collected and ground up by diamond tools for use as diamond grit on the sawing and faceting machines.

Next comes the faceting of the stone. In the old days faceting was not the highly scientific process it is today. In those days the facets were frequently produced by a chipping method and the stones lacked the beauty and fire given by modern cutting methods. The Koh-i-noor diamond, for instance, when first brought to this country was very inexpertly cut, and though it lost a good deal of weight when it was recut it gained immensely in beauty to become one of the glories of the British Crown Jewels.

Faceting has been brought to a fine art. The object of cutting facets is to trap the light rays which reflect from the cut surface. The facets are so arranged that the light rays striking through the top of the stone are reflected back by the under facets and emerge again through the top ones. During this process the ray of ordinary white light is split up into all the colours of the spectrum. Anyone wearing a diamond can watch these light rays flashing with ever-changing variety.

Most people think of the diamond in these terms—as a clear, colourless stone, and certainly the clearer and the whiter it is the greater its value and beauty. Occasionally, however, diamonds with a very pronounced colour are found and these are both valuable and very beautiful. Some of these are described in the chapter on famous gems.

Because of its value, as well as for other obvious reasons, it is very necessary to know some of the points to look for when choosing a diamond. De Beers Consolidated Mines have drawn up what is virtually a 'Charter for Choosing a Diamond'. In this they describe the four simple 'C' clues to diamond values: Carat-weight, Colour, Clarity, and Cut.

1. Carat-weight

The weight of a diamond is assessed in carats. There are 142 carats to the ounce. Diamonds of above 3 carats are becoming increasingly rare and prices therefore rise sharply with carat-weight. A stone of 4 carats, for example, is valued at considerably more than twice a 2 carat diamond of similar quality.

2. Colour

Diamonds are not always white. They come in many lovely shades—pale yellow, coffee brown, red, pink, green blue, even black. The Dresden diamond, one of the Saxon Crown Jewels, is apple green. Traditionally, however, the standard for the engagement ring is a clear, frosty sparkling white. This is not the so-called 'blue-white', but more like the white drops of spray that shine through the cascade of a waterfall. Diamonds with any tinge of blue in them are very rare. But diamonds do reflect the colour around them. To judge its colour, look at a diamond on a white background against a clear north light.

3. Clarity

A diamond is considered to be 'flawless' if no flaws are visible to the trained eye when the diamond is magnified ten times. Other diamonds are valued according to the number, kind and location of the 'inclusions'—minute imperfections such as fissures, bubbles, black carbon specks and other impurities—that are revealed by a detailed examination. In many cases these inclusions do not affect the beauty of the stone as seen by the naked eye; but they do affect the price.

4. Cut

Whatever the colour and clarity of a diamond, only fine cutting can reveal its full beauty. Each diamond must be shaped and the surface faceted so as to catch each beam of light. When light enters a polished diamond it is refracted, broken up into all the colours of the spectrum and reflected back through the top surface. But these rainbow flashes occur only if the diamond is properly cut. It is the quality of the cutting which enhances the value of each diamond.

Of all Nature's treasures the diamond is probably the most lasting. No matter through how many generations it may be handed down, its pristine beauty will remain undimmed.

But it is not only because of its beauty as a gemstone that the diamond is prized; it is also the most useful and indispensable of all precious stones. Without diamonds our industries could never have progressed as they have and we would be without many of the comforts and refinements which have raised our standards of life throughout the years. Aircraft and motor-car industries use an immense amount of industrial diamonds, essential to high-precision work; they are used on metal disc saws to cut through certain rocks, and crushed boart (as the inferior type of industrial diamond is described), mixed with oil, is used to polish the hardest surfaces. Radios, television sets, telephones, vacuum cleaners—the list of modern developments of which industrial diamonds are an important part is endless. The diamond can truly be said to be at once the most beautiful and the most strikingly useful of all gems.

II. Emeralds

Emeralds of size and intense green tint are undoubtedly gems of great beauty—and value. Cleopatra's magnificent jewels included not only some of the world's finest diamonds but also a profusion of emeralds from her own mines—an admirable foil for her famous auburn hair. History shows that these gems have always been favoured by red-haired women, who rightly regarded them as undoubtedly most becoming to their Titian colouring. Napoleon III was reputed to have presented the Empress Eugénie with an emerald 'clover-leaf' sparkling with diamond 'dewdrops' after she had admired a real clover-leaf during an afternoon walk with the Emperor, and soon after her marriage the City of Paris presented her with a wonderful diadem of emeralds as a wedding gift.

Some of the world's finest emeralds come from the famous Mozo mines in Colombia, which have had a very chequered history. From producing many thousands of dollars worth of fine emeralds each year the mines ceased entirely to be worked until, in 1947, the Colombia Government took them over, only to discontinue working them two years later. It was not until the early 1950's that a chance discovery of a rich deposit of emeralds set the miners digging again. Miners work on 'shelves' at the sides of steep cliffs and search for the emeralds under the constantly watchful eyes of armed guards—a necessary precaution, for a mere handful of the emeralds can well prove to be worth a vast fortune. When they have been mined the rough emeralds are sent to the capital, Bogotá, where they are sorted and graded and from whence they go to merchants throughout the world. The market is virtually a state-controlled one in that the supply is temporarily withheld if there are signs of a surplus holding.

Russia has its emerald mines but the gems found there, though large, lack the vivid green of the Colombian-mined gems, having a more yellowish undertone. Brazil, Australia and South Africa also produce emeralds but again of a lighter green tone. In 1956 an emerald weighing a reputed 11 lb. was found in the latter country on a hilltop in the Letaba district of the Transvaal. The stone broke as it was extracted but the broken piece, measuring 8 in. × 3 in., was reported to be of good quality and, at a weight of $141\frac{3}{4}$ carats, well may be one of the largest in the world, though the Devonshire emerald is 161 carats. One of the finest known emeralds hitherto is said to weigh 136 carats and formerly belonged to the Tsars of Russia. It is now presumably among the vast treasures of the Soviet Government.

Emeralds from the Sandawana deposit near Belingwe are very

THE FIVE PRECIOUS GEMS

fine and it is appropriate that some of these wonderful gems were given to H.M. Queen Elizabeth the Queen Mother when, in May 1960, she visited the first Central African Trade Fair which she officially opened.

These six emeralds are said to be the purest and therefore among the most beautiful in the world. They were dug up with a garden fork, it is reported, about fifty miles south-east of Bulawayo. At about $1,500 a carat for flawless, top-quality emeralds these six perfect gems must be well worth a 'Queen's ransom'. The rarity of fine emeralds of true colour keeps their value high so that they remain, like diamonds, a good investment as well as a thing of beauty and a joy for ever.

Colombian emeralds are distinguished, as well as by their wonderful green colouring, by their comparative clearness and six-sided prisms. Belonging to the beryl group, true emeralds get their colour from the presence of chromic oxide. The clear green of the Colombian emerald is absent to a large degree from those found in the Australian deposits, in which the colour is somewhat clouded. Sometimes emeralds are imitated by the process of placing a thin layer of green between slices of colourless quartz which have the natural feathery markings of real emeralds. Sometimes, too, the appearance of a large emerald is achieved by cementing two slices of real emerald together to make a larger stone. Sometimes crackled quartz dyed green is used to imitate emerald. A gem-testing laboratory is the proper testing ground for any emerald about which doubt may be felt, the highly technical instruments plus the expert distinguishing the true worth of the gems.

Emeralds, like rubies and sapphires, are not usually very heavily faceted. To begin with, they may be cracked or fractured and they can be irreparably damaged by a sharp blow. In spite of this, they are often engraved and carved, even today. In some particularly fine jewels where emeralds are used to simulate leaves in a flower spray for example, the veining of the leaf is achieved by engraving. Queen Mary owned a very beautiful engraved emerald which she sometimes wore as a pendant. This was a gift from India when she attended the Coronation Durbar with her husband, George V. The gift had a special significance for the Queen apart from its beauty; being born in May under the sign of Gemini the emerald was her birthstone.

Step-cutting is the favourite method of cutting emeralds—so much so that this form of cutting has become known as emerald-cut even when used for cutting diamonds, particularly for solitaire rings. Emerald cutting produces an oblong- or a square-shaped stone with facets polished diagonally across the corners. Brilliant and rose cutting, used so much for diamonds, especially the smaller ones, are less frequently used for emeralds. Completely smooth and domed emeralds are described as being cut *en cabochon*, and it is in this form that they are, perhaps, most beautiful.

III. Sapphires

It is no poetical flight of fancy to describe those regions which once comprised the British Empire as being studded with sapphires, those beautiful deep-blue gems which help to make some of the jewels of history as well as of this modern age. Ceylon, Burma, Siam and the Vale of Kashmir are sources of the most valuable sapphires, while from Australia come sapphires of deep indigo and deep greenish blue.

Although the name 'sapphire' immediately conjures up a picture of a deep-blue gem, sapphires of almost every primary colour are found in both Ceylon and Burma—yellow sapphires, green sapphires, violet sapphires, as well as sapphires in pink, white and a tawny sherry shade. White sapphires are extremely rare and, to the uninitiated, should be suspect as synthetic.

Sapphires of the same dense indigo-blue as the Australian variety are also found in Fergus County, Montana, while the Yogo Gulch has yielded sapphires of blue and magenta tints. Madagascar sapphires include rough crystals of an almost navy-blue shade. The most beautiful, in the opinion of many, are the unique gems known as asteria or star-sapphires which are usually cloudy and somewhat pale in colour. Like the star-ruby, owing to a peculiar formation of the crystal, these gems reveal a six-pointed star of light, most clearly seen when they are viewed from above. For this reason, to show the star-formation to the best advantage, star-sapphires are usually cut *en cabochon*, with a high rounded dome and perfectly smooth. A feature of the star-sapphire, as with the star-ruby, is that a complete star is always seen in each separate piece even if the gem is cut into several pieces.

Chemically, the sapphire is twin to the ruby of the same species—corundum—and in its pure state is a clear, colourless stone. Its colour (and that of the ruby) is due to the minute particles of iron, chromium or titanium oxides in varying quantities present in the corundum. It is for this reason that the colour of the ruby and the sapphire varies according to geographical conditions. In Ceylon, however, corundum stones have been found which have both red and blue in the same crystal.

Though the different methods of cutting sapphires vary, they are generally step- or trap-cut in the same way as emeralds —square or oblong with triangular corners when a large stone is concerned. They are, too, often cut *en cabochon*. Smaller sapphires are frequently baguette cut, particularly where they are used to 'build up' a solid design such as the massed background to a badge of office or a jewelled order—a form known as pavé. Because the colour of sapphires is sometimes somewhat patchy the stone has to be cut with great care. This is necessary, too, because the colour varies according to the direction in which the light travels through the gem owing to the property in some doubly-refractive stones called dichroism.

Native cutting—still done in Ceylon—is generally easily recognizable by the often unsymmetrical, if clever, cutting. This affects the colour of the stone, and for European tastes it becomes necessary to recut it, resulting naturally in some reduction of its size. For while the native cutting was aimed at retaining the size of the sapphire, European cutters, or lapidaries, were—and are— more concerned with conserving perfection of colour even at the cost of losing some of the weight of the stone. By keeping surface cutting to a minimum lapidaries can retain a greater depth of colour and so achieve true artistic perfection.

In spite of its hardness, the sapphire is frequently carved, particularly in the case of gems to be used as seals, or when the sapphires are used to represent the petals of a flower in a jewelled spray or cluster brooch.

Sapphires, quite rightly, have a place of honour in the British Crown Jewels, but their symbolical value as the gems of virtue, constancy and truth, apart from their intrinsic beauty has made sapphires favourite stones for other ceremonial regalia. The famous Golden Rose, which was blessed by the Pope on the fourth Sunday in Lent and then sent to a distinguished person, church or community, was of wrought gold set with sapphires. Pope Innocent III, *circa* 1198–1216, decreed that the Bishop's Ring should take the form of a sapphire set in gold.

Though these historical sapphires were set in gold, the modern gem is usually set in platinum. One of the loveliest combinations of gems is that of sapphires flanked by emeralds—a perfect colour scheme of Nature's finest devising.

IV. RUBIES

Red glowing rubies have a great beauty which makes them very desirable as jewels but, since the mines in Burma which were the source of the world's finest gems have virtually ceased to be worked, they have scarcity value too.

Seldom large, the ruby varies in its colour from one mining country to another. Those from the ruby mines of Burma (the largest of which ceased to be mined in 1925) are considerèd to be the finest. Of rich, deep red, these rubies have no trace of the saturated brownish tinge which often distinguishes the otherwise equally red Siamese ruby and brings it more nearly to the colour of an almadine garnet. Ceylon rubies, while lacking the deep red of the Burmese or Siamese rubies, are compensated by having more life and sparkle than the two former gems. Like the sapphire, rubies are of the corundum mineral species, basically of the same structure and differentiated chiefly only in colour. Like the sapphire, too, rubies are sometimes found with an inherent six-pointed star shape within. Such species are called star, or asteria, rubies and sapphires.

Second only in hardness to a diamond, the real Burma 'pigeon's blood' ruby is rare and very valuable and anyone acquiring or owning such a stone has a great treasure if it is of any size. In buying a reputed Burmese ruby it is necessary to be very sure of its genuineness. In the real gem there are inescapable evidences of inner irregularities formed by Nature alone, particularly some fine needle-like spines, known to the gemmologist as 'silk' because of the silky effect they have when seen through a microscope. In synthetic gems the lens will usually reveal air bubbles and regularly curved lines caused by the building-up of the stones by artificial means. In the real Burma ruby there are sometimes patches of a deeper red and these alone are usually sufficient guarantee of the origin and worth of the stone—they are Nature's hand-print and so far incapable of simulation by man.

Because their beauty lies in their rich red colour with no light refraction introduced by the intricate cutting which gives the diamond its full brilliance, rubies are step- or trap-cut and sometimes *en cabochon*, i.e. domed or rounded on the top. In some jewellery they are polished in the form of a complete sphere, drilled and threaded like beads, the strings graduated like those of a pearl necklace, or twisted like a rope. Sometimes the *cabochon* cutting of rubies is adopted when they are small, or have slight imperfections. Sometimes they are interspersed with similar spheres of emeralds or sapphires into fashionably casual-seeming, but enormously expensive necklaces and matching bracelets—a conceit much liked by the more fabulous jewellers of Paris and Rome in particular. Sometimes rows of ruby 'beads' are used, with diamond baguettes between, to make an apparently simple bracelet which may well run into four figures.

Usually, when a fine red ruby is used for a ring it is either flanked by a baguette diamond at either side or completely surrounded by diamonds, the fire of which enhances the lovely dark red of the ruby. Even when a ruby is faceted, this is kept to the minimum, the brittleness of the stone (notwithstanding its hardness it *is* a somewhat brittle stone) militating against too much cutting, apart from aesthetic considerations.

As an example of the present-day value of rubies of any size, records show that one of eight carats—about the size of the ordinary garden pea—was sold at Christie's, in London, recently for the world record price of $60,000, or $7,500 a carat. At the same sale a ruby and diamond brooch realized nearly $12,000.

V. Pearls

Pearls, like the oysters which create them, are perhaps an acquired taste. Their attraction and real beauty is something which grows. The pearl is a gem for the connoisseur and a quest for the collector. With the development of the cultured pearl industry and the perfecting of deceptively 'good' looking artificial pearls there has been a tendency to relegate the real pearl to those for whom 'only the best will do'. To the fastidious, and to the connoisseur, however, pearls have an enormous appeal and many years and many thousands of dollars will be spent by them in the collection of perfectly matched pearls for a necklace.

Pearls seem to have an historical tradition in Britain. The crowns of the early Saxon kings were set with pearls, while the Imperial State Crown in the British Crown Jewels holds four immense pear-shaped pearls which are said to have been worn by the Tudor Queen Elizabeth I as ear-rings. Certainly exactly similar pearls are shown being worn by the Queen in several contemporary paintings. A portrait of Queen Margaret of Scotland, wife of James IV, shows her wearing a long girdle composed of massive ropes of pearls, as well as a handsome pearl bracelet.

Returning Crusaders brought back with them vast quantities of pearls among their spoils of war—so many, indeed, that their ladies not only wore them as rope necklaces, but had them sewn in intricate patterns all over their voluminous robes. Even so, there were still many gems over and these the ingenious wives had sewn on their little caps in a fascinating lattice-work pattern.

But the full flowering of pearls at the British Court occurred in Tudor times when long, flowing veils and head-dresses were richly spangled with large pearls; when the armholes of dresses were outlined with pearls; and when they were frequently sewn into closely packed rows to form literal collars of pearls. The Tudor Queen Elizabeth happily continued the fashion when she succeeded to the throne and it is recorded that she paid the then vast sum of £3,000 for the pearls which Mary, Queen of Scots had received as a gift from her mother, Catherine de' Medici.

An equally lavish use of pearls as personal and as dress ornaments characterized the sixteenth and seventeenth centuries. The fashion was not confined to women alone, for when the Duke of Buckingham visited Paris in order to bring back Henrietta Maria to be the bride of Charles I, he wore a suitably impressive ensemble of rich purple satin lavishly embroidered with pearls which were said to be valued—even in those days—at £20,000. So through the centuries that followed, even through the rise, fall and restoration of the monarchy, pearls remained a firm favourite, perhaps on account of their deceptively simple and modest air. Queen Victoria maintained the royal liking for these gems and owned many lovely examples of pearl jewellery.

The fascination of pearls is understandable because they are among the most elusive of gems—a good catch in one season may be followed by a very poor catch in the next. A good example of this contrariness is the record of a government estimate in the last century of an oyster population of a famous pearling locality as 16,000,000, yet a few months later not a single oyster was to be found there. This happens time and again. Then again one oyster may yield nothing; another may yield a pearl worth a fortune. It is seldom that an oyster will yield more than one, or perhaps two or three, though there are records of an oyster which contained eighty-seven pearls and of another, fished in Ceylon, which contained sixty-seven smaller pearls.

The colour and quality of pearls varies very much according to the locality in which they are found. In the Persian Gulf and Ceylon the pearls are distinguished by a fine creamy colour—true 'Orient'—though some found in Ceylon have a faintly rose-pink tinge and others a slightly yellow hue. Pearls from the West Indian seas are sometimes of a deep rose colour, while others may have a yellowish tint. Black pearls, those sought-after and richly prized gems, are found chiefly in the Gulf of Mexico and in the waters around some of the Pacific Islands. Australian pearls are perhaps the whitest, with a silvery sheen, and are probably the largest found. Venezuelan pearls can be clear white or a pale golden yellow—in fact, a pearl expert can usually name the source of a pearl from its colour alone.

As diamonds are sorted into groups and sold through a central selling agency, so pearls are graded in sizes and colours and sold, to a great extent, through the pearl markets of the East. Here the pearls are divided into groups, with white, cream and pink-tinted pearls forming the main ones. Other colours, which may include grey, mauve and deep creamy-yellow, will be grouped together as 'miscellaneous'.

When the pearls have been sorted for colour they are then graded for size, the small round ones of less than a grain going into the 'seed' pearl group. Larger pearls are carefully drilled and strung on three- or four-inch lengths of silk, each length holding pearls of similar size and colour. Several of these strings are then bunched together and finished off with a decorative cord or coloured metal swag ready for the buyers' inspection. From these markets the pearls go all over the world, with the finest bound for London, Paris, New York and, latterly, Italy—the recognized pearl customers of Europe. From the pearl merchant they pass to the jeweller, from him to the pearl stringer and mounter, finally finding their way to the velvet- or silk-lined jewel-case.

Sometimes the buyers in the pearl markets are concerned only with the acquisition of a few pearls of a specific size and colour to match up a necklace which is being formed. It has been known to take fifteen to twenty years to complete the collection of pearls for a perfectly matched, perfectly graded necklace. Small wonder, then, that such a jewel may cost the eventual owner some hundreds of thousands of dollars to acquire.

This is true even of the finer cultured pearls, for though the 'seed' may be planted artificially, only Nature will determine the colouring, shape and size of the ultimate pearl. It can therefore be as difficult to achieve a perfectly matched string of cultured pearls as of real ones, the only difference being that with artificially induced pearls the number available is naturally greater and more predictable than those of Nature's own conception, than which nothing is lovelier nor more desirable. Even though a cultured pearl is 'real' in the sense that it grows, it yet cannot compare with the natural real pearl, lovely though it may be. A point to bear in mind when considering the cost of a real pearl against that of a cultured one (which has its own validity and beauty) is that with real pearls the removal of one or more layers from a pearl of bad colour to reveal a less discoloured surface below is possible and is accepted practice. So, too, when very old pearls show signs of wear they can be restored to perfect shape and lustre by exposing a lower concentric layer. But with a cultured pearl these processes are not possible because the removal of the outer layers of pearl matter will eventually bring one to the bead or core of mother of pearl. The importance of this is recognized by the practices of the Federal Trade Commission, which states, *inter alia*, that it must be correctly disclosed when pearls are cultured—and that imitation pearls may not be sold as either cultured or real.

The valuation of pearls takes into account, apart from the hazards undergone in their fishing and scarcity, the beauty of their colour, their form and regularity (pitting, denting and other blemishes lower their value) and the size, which is usually expressed in terms of weight. This is assessed in grains, one grain equalling one-quarter carat or one-twentieth of a gramme.

Perfectly spherical pearls are the ideal for necklaces, and the larger the pearl the more valuable it is since there are far fewer large than small pearls recovered from the oysters. Drop- and pear-shaped pearls are used chiefly as additions to a necklace proper, either of pearls or diamonds. Princess Alexandra wears a necklace from which hang five pear-shaped pearls—a perfect example of this style. Very often a pair of pear-shaped pearls is used to form a pair of ear-rings, but the matching needed for these is a long and arduous—and often costly—task. Sometimes the nucleus of the pearl adheres to the oyster shell, producing a pearl with a domed top and a flat back. These are known as 'button' or *bouton* pearls and are chiefly used for solitaire rings, stud ear-rings and set in brooches and bracelets with other gems. Blister pearls are malformations, too, and are sometimes quite hollow. In the case of button pearls the hole drilled before selling is usually made only half-way through the pearl so as to admit the 'spike' on which it will be fixed in the final piece of jewellery.

'Deformed' pearls, described as 'baroque', are oddities, like potatoes that grow into queer shapes and are as equally incapable of explanation. Such pearls have offered jewellery designers endless scope for ingenuity in forming the misshapen pearl into a unique jewel. One of the most notable of these is the famous Canning jewel, in which a large baroque pearl forms the torso of a mythological figure. There are many such examples, some of great antiquity, showing that the jewellers of the past, like those of the present, were alive to the challenge presented by these freaks of Nature.

River or freshwater pearls are sometimes (but somewhat rarely) found in the mountain streams and tarns of the northern hemisphere, from such rivers as the Spey, the South Esk, the Forth, the Teith and the Tay in Scotland. Twelve pearls of differing sizes found in the last-named river were formed into a brooch of floral and fern design, with white and yellow gold and amethyst, and presented to Queen Elizabeth II when she visited Perth to open the Queen's Bridge in October 1960. Queen Victoria is believed to have owned pearls taken from pearl-bearing mussels found in Scottish waters.

North Wales, too, has had its pearl fisheries, some of which are still 'worked'. At one time the River Conway was famed for its pearls and there is good authority for the belief that a pearl from this river is in one of the British crowns, having been presented by Sir Richard Wynn. Some of the rivers of Ireland, too, have produced pearls, notably the rivers of Wexford, Tyrone and Donegal. River pearls are also found in Saxony, Bavaria, and Czechoslovakia, as well as in many parts of the United States. They have been systematically 'worked' in the Little Miami River, Warren County, Ohio, as well as on the Mississippi, notably about Muscatine, Iowa.

Because these freshwater pearls lack the true oriental lustre they are usually much whiter in colour, with less translucence, though with a silvery sheen. The River Irt in Cumberland was once a source of pearls, and William Camden, a contemporary of the Tudor Queen Elizabeth, wrote of the pearl fishing there, 'In this brook, the shell fish eagerly sucking in the dew, conceive and bring forth pearls', giving further support to the legend that pearls were 'solidified dew-drops'.

One of the characteristics of the pearl which particularly endears it to women is the fact that the appearance of pearls is enhanced if they are worn constantly. Pearls seem to establish a close personal link with the wearer and in olden times people believed that pearls were alive and were nourished by contact with the skin of the wearer. If neglected they lost their lustre and were said to have 'sickened'. It is a strange fact that when some of the ancient Egyptian tombs were opened other jewels which were buried in the sarcophagi had remained unchanged, but the pearls so buried crumbled away at a touch. Pearls do need to be worn, for if they are stored away their lustre is indeed dimmed. Fortunately the pearl is one of the most accommodating of jewels and any woman who is fortunate enough to possess pearls can wear them with fashion 'rightness' at any time and on any occasion.

CHAPTER TWO

Some gemstones

AFTER the five primary precious stones come the colourful semi-precious (or more correctly, gemstones), each with a charm and validity of its own and placed into a different category by reason of its comparably lower intrinsic value alone.

The opal, of these gemstones, is perhaps one of the most varied in its colouring, showing all the hues of the rainbow, yet with little colour of its own. Truly a paradox of a gem, of which the lapidary's description seems cold in comparison with the hidden fire of the gem. 'It is a form of silica,' the expert writes, 'with an amount of water varying from six to ten per cent in precious opal. It differs from the other principal gemstones in that it is not a crystal, but a kind of solidified jelly. The characteristic display of colour in the opal is the essence of its beauty and its opalescence results from the fact that as the jelly (the opal material deposited from natural hot waters or hot springs) cools, it hardens and loses part of its original water. This process of solidifying produces cracks, which may become filled with other opal material.'

The lapidary's precise description of this elusively beautiful stone goes on to describe how this new opal has a different refractive index if it contains even a slightly different amount of water, but becomes more lyrical as he points out that the layers thus built up reflect the light rays in such a way that they interfere, producing the colours associated with soap bubbles, oil on water, 'and rainbows'. Thus the poetical note creeps in which can hardly be absent from an attempt to describe a gemstone that holds within it every pure colour. Thickness and uniformity of the layers and the direction in which they are viewed in fact determine the opal's particular 'colour', the minute cracks which split up the light as it strikes the stone giving shades of great purity and intensity. Opals vary in their primary colour; there are the black, white and the fire opal in addition to the common

30

opals which lack any play of colour. The differentiation in opals is fascinating; the white opal actually has flecked colours of great purity against a light background, either of white or tinted a pale yellow or pink. What gives the black opal its name is its dark background, the description of 'black' opal being something of a misnomer because it is generally milky-blue or grey. The fire opal has a great deal of opalescence, is more transparent and has a red, orange or yellow background, giving it its fire.

Opal is a mineral which is virtually amorphous, growing in irregular shapes in the cavities of rocks, or coating the surfaces of other minerals—even replacing them.

Black opals, found only in the famous Lightning Ridge fields in New South Wales, are, because of their scarcity, among the rarest of gems. Some of the most spectacular have been given individual names, after the manner of famous diamonds, and are, in the main, now in the U.S.A. The first black opals were found in New South Wales in 1889, when a hunter trailing a wounded kangaroo picked up a fine specimen and so led to the discovery of the rich deposits there. In 1905 the fabulous Lightning Ridge Field with its black opals was discovered. Later on further discoveries of opal deposits in Queensland produced a fine supply of black opals.

The United States became an opal producer when a find of black opals was made in Humboldt County, Nevada. Many fine opals were taken from that field, including the magnificent Roebling opal, now in the United States National Museum in Washington. Though these opals from Nevada are very beautiful, they have one drawback—they tend to develop very fine cracks when exposed to the atmosphere unless they are specially treated.

Flame-red or orange-tinted fire opals, with the opalescence hidden deep down in the stone by the overall red to yellow colouring have been found in Mexico, but these supplies are said now to be exhausted. One type of common opal shows its opalescence only after it has been immersed in water; other varieties of common opal resemble chalcedony.

An opal of peculiarly potent attraction is the Mexican water opal—the one variety of opal which it is impossible successfully to imitate. As one views the stone from different angles, lovely flashes of vivid and differing colours come from the depth of the gem.

As with emeralds, opals are sometimes made into doublets. Two or more pieces are cemented to make a composite gem, a doublet containing two pieces of opal cemented or fused together, while triplets have three pieces so joined. These composite gems can consist entirely of genuine stones, or they may be a combination of real and imitation. The cementing or fusing is done before the gems are cut.

In general, opals are cut *en cabochon*, with a domed surface in varying grades of steepness. The steepest dome is used for rings and the flatter domed shape for brooches, pendants and bracelets. This form of cutting is used for most opals except the fire opal, which are the only ones faceted. Opals are generally delicate gems and need the greatest care in handling, hence the *cabochon* cut in the majority of cases.

Some opals will absorb grease when the polished surface has become worn, 'breathing it in' as it were, and in consequence will become dulled. Heat, much more than dryness, is its enemy and because of the peculiar nature of its structure an opal is particularly susceptible to the effect of excessive artificial heating and can be damaged beyond repair if kept near heat.

Opal matrix is the combined opal and surrounding stone cluster in which it is found which has to be cut scientifically to reveal the pure opal within.

Recently opals have come again into the gem news because of a big new strike at Lightning Ridge, but it is unlikely that the yield will be of sufficient quantity to upset the market—chiefly because the find does not include any notable black opals which can, and presumably always will, command high prices—more from buyers in the United States and Japan than from those in Australia.

Amber was once regarded as a precious stone. Unlike mined

The Cullinan in the rough and the four largest stones cut from it. The biggest portion, the Star of Africa, is now in the British Queen's sceptre.

A diamond embedded in a piece of rock.

This diamond was found in the gravel of the Woyie River, Sierra Leone, in 1945. Weighing 770 carats it is exceeded in size only by the Cullinan (3,106 carats) and the Excelsior (995 carats). It is the largest *alluvial* diamond ever found.

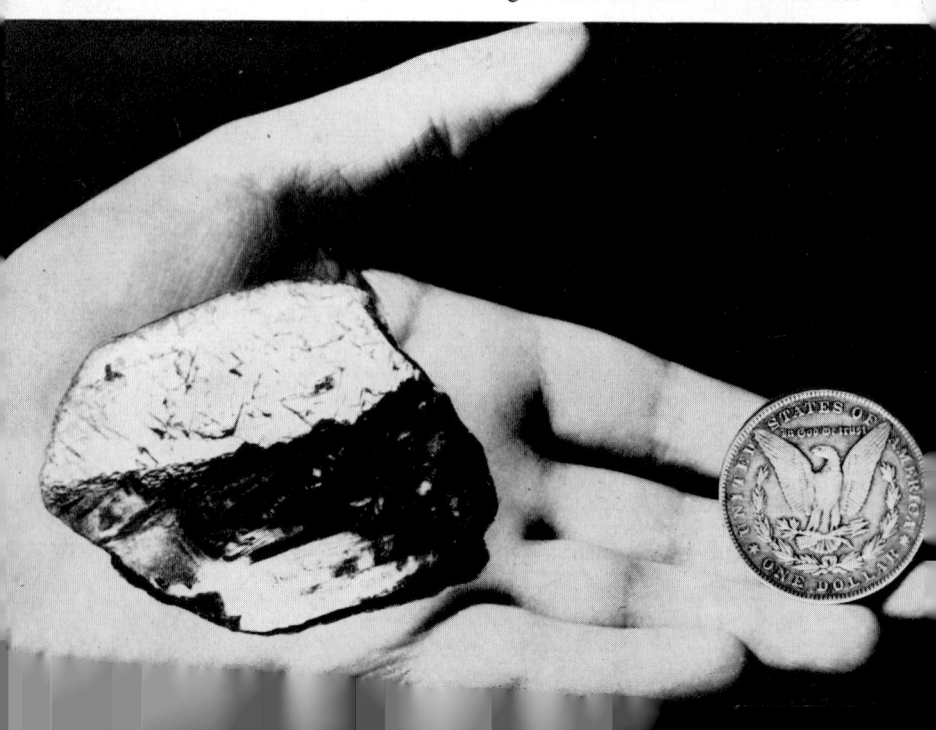

This is the celebrated Hope blue diamond displayed today in the Smithsonian Institution, Washington. The late owner, Mrs. Evalyn Walsh McLean, wore the jewel for decades as it is seen here, suspended on a necklace of forty-six white diamonds of oddly assorted cuts and shapes. The Hope is as blue as a sapphire and weighs 44½ carats.

Pearls were the favourite jewels of Queen Elizabeth. In this portrait the Queen is seen wearing her pearl necklaces and a pearl-studded crown. Her gown is richly embroidered with pearls and other gems. (By courtesy of the British National Portrait Gallery.)

gems, it is a fossilized resin which has oozed from immense conifers of millions of years ago, much of it washed up on many shores, notably those of the Baltic Sea. From this latter source the amber is usually in shades of light yellow, orange and brown. Amber from Rumania is in the same tones, while that from China and Burma has yellow and reddish-brown tints. Not all amber, however, is washed up: in the East Prussia region, for instance, there are mines from which amber in all its many lovely hues from pale yellow to mahogany reddish brown are excavated. No one appears to have advanced a reason why some forms of amber are cloudy and others not. In all its variations amber is one of the most fascinating of gemstones, deservedly making a return to popular fashion. In these days of synthetics it is useful to know that the real thing can be distinguished by two simple tests—real amber is of incredible lightness in weight, and it has a slightly electrical property. To test the presence of the latter, rub a piece of amber over the palm of the hand and then hold the amber over a small piece of tissue paper. A genuine piece of amber will pick up the paper as a magnet does a metal object. A feature of real amber is that it is a 'living' organism and will change its colour and its sheen with age.

Amethyst—another gemstone which is returning to fashion—belongs to the crystallized quartz group and comes into the category of gemstones rather than precious stones because of the plentiful supply, though at one time the amethyst was esteemed above the diamond (in the far-off days before diamonds began to be cut and polished). In its true purple colouring it is a most attractive gemstone, much used for jewellery in Victorian times, when it was set in gold and usually surrounded by pearls in brooches, rings, necklaces and ear-rings. The quartz is found in the Urals, in Ceylon, and in Brazil and Uruguay, and is most often faceted.

Aquamarines are today regarded more as a precious than as a gemstone and command quite a high price. Their beauty is retained in all the loveliness of colour and translucence under artificial light. Belonging to the beryl family like the emerald, they have a low refractivity of light, the value and appearance depending on flawlessness, purity of colour, and size. Usually the aquamarine is step-cut in rectangular form. This most appropriately named of all gemstones is most prized in the pale sea-blue shade; in the greenish tones it is not so much sought after and is less seldom used for jewellery in the higher price range. Aquamarines are found in Russia—in the Urals—in South Africa, Ceylon, the United States, in India, and, of course, in Brazil where the stones are usually of very fine quality and colour, and where one of the largest aquamarines ever found was discovered. This measured 19 in. × 16 in. and was found early in the present century. Nothing comparable to this has ever been found in any of the other sources.

Whilst the sea-blue or sea-green **beryl** is rightly called an aquamarine, the gem is also found in a rose-pink and red shades, when it is described as morganite; and in a golden-yellow colour, known as heliodor. The mineral composition is the same, the colour determining into which category of description the gem belongs.

Cornelian is a chalcedony and is found in a beefy-red or orange-red colour, generally used in men's signet rings, or in the form of polished beads for a necklace. It was sometimes used as a large central stone in Victorian brooches but has never been a really popular gem.

Citrine, because of its yellow colour and general appearance, is sometimes confused with and sold as topaz. It is a yellow quartz (the purple quartz being called the amethyst) and is, in fact, sometimes produced from the amethyst quartz by subjecting it to heat treatment which results in different shading according to the amount of heat applied. In its natural state, the yellow tones of the citrine vary, like the topaz, from pale sherry yellow to the deep, brownish yellow of dark sherry. It is often called golden quartz.

Garnets owe their name to the Latin word meaning pomegranate, which is very descriptive both of the colour of the ripe fruit and of the gemstone. The red variety of garnets are called pyrope garnets but they are found in many other colours, too, coming mostly from South Africa and North America, though some have been found in England, in Westmorland and the Lake District in particular. But the garnet most used in Victorian times comes from Bohemia—of a rich, dark red, though garnets of an equally good red colour come from Arizona and Kimberley. Another variety is the almadine garnet, found in several parts of the world, chiefly in Brazil, Uruguay, India, Ceylon, the United States and Australia. The carbuncle of Victorian times was actually a deep red garnet cut *en cabochon*, deeply domed and hollowed underneath. In this form the garnet was used as a large central stone in the girandole brooch and in single-stone rings, sometimes with a star or with pearls superimposed on the surface of the dome.

Jet, it is claimed, was first found in Whitby, Yorkshire, where the cutting and polishing of this hard black ligneous substance was a local family craft, now fast dying out. Like coal and amber it is a fossil, and enjoyed its heyday in the nineteenth century when it was used profusely for elegantly carved and faceted necklaces, bracelets, ear-rings and brooches. Today it is usually lightened by being used in combination with crystal beads.

Moonstones belong to the feldspar family and are one of the least expensive of the gemstones, despite their attractive milky-blue tint, exactly the colour of well-skimmed milk. Each stone has a subtle line of light through it which moves as the stone is moved. This vagrant light ray has been likened to a moonbeam which is probably the source of its name—moonstone. Found in Ceylon, it is never faceted and is mostly used in small circular shapes to make necklets and bracelets, and more rarely rings.

Peridots are sometimes called olivines—a name which more nearly describes the gemstone in its yellowish-green colour. Most peridots, however, are of a leaf green or a darker, bottle green. The main source of these attractive gemstones is the Island of St. John in the Red Sea, though they are also found in Australia and in Burma. The demantoid garnet, which is a green garnet, is sometimes wrongly described as a peridot.

Topaz is a gem which was much loved by the Victorians, one which is once again in high fashion as well it might be, for its fascinating range of colourings through all the shades of yellow, from pale to dark sherry brown, make it an attractive and adaptable gem, even if it is not among the primary precious stones.

As well as the 'sherry' tones, topaz is found in other colours —in white, pink and blue, bluey-green and even in a rich red. The clear colourless stones are picturesquely named by the Brazilians *pingos d'agoa*—drops of water. But most of the topaz from Brazil are of a deep brown shade and in order to make them more appealing in appearance the gems are subjected artificially to a great heat which has the effect of turning them from their original brown colour to a delightful rose-pink. The sherry-yellow crystals of topaz which in the past have been extensively used in jewellery were almost all from the neighbourhood of Ouro Preto in Brazil.

Other sources of the gemstone include the Urals, Siberia, Ceylon, Madagascar, Burma, Japan, America (Connecticut) and Australia, the most frequently occurring varieties being the golden-yellow and tawny coloured stones. At the beginning of the present century, however, a remarkably fine dark-blue topaz was found in Ceylon. It was of considerable size and even after cutting weighed more than 350 carats.

Topaz from the Urals and Nerchinsk in Siberia are usually of a pale blue and bluey-green, in many cases almost indistinguishable in appearance from the delicate aquamarine. Perhaps the most beautiful of all the varieties is the rare rose-topaz, a soft rose-pink stone with a hint of lilac in it. The gemstone's name is often wrongly applied to other gemstones, i.e. the 'Oriental Topaz' is actually the yellow sapphire, and the 'Scotch Topaz' is the cairngorm, a variety of quartz.

Again, fine topaz is quite frequently confused with the yellow citrine—a clear yellow variety of transparent quartz. Usually the prefix 'Brazilian' to a topaz will establish it as a genuine topaz and not a citrine.

Tourmalines are fascinating gemstones of comparatively recent emergence. They are found in many colours, some of these appearing in one stone shading from pink to brown and from green to pink, or having an inner colour different from the outer, main colour. Some are found in the green characteristic of an emerald and, indeed, Brazilian tourmalines of this decided green tint were sometimes shipped from Brazil as 'Brazilian emeralds'. Sources of these stones include the United States, Ceylon, Brazil and Russia.

The present liking for colourful jewellery has brought back into favour one of the oldest known gemstones—the **Turquoise.** Its name alone has come to connote a pure sky-blue, but in truth this stone has for centuries been prized not only for that beautiful colour but also for its supposed magical properties. In the remote valleys of Yarkand and Thibet the turquoise is hung around the neck of a favourite pony to ward off the evil eye. In that precipitous mountain terrain, on many of whose paths a slip would mean instant death, faith is still placed in the turquoise to keep the animal's feet from slipping.

A treatise written on the turquoise in the thirteenth century asserts: 'Whoever owns the true turquoise set in gold will not injure any of his limbs when he falls, whether he be riding or walking, so long as he has the stone with him.' The Apache Indians of North America considered that a bow tipped with turquoise, or a gun studded with this beautiful blue stone, is an infallible weapon, the turquoise being supposed to render the owner's aim unerring. It was said to ensure fidelity in a loved one, while Persian men would constantly wear a large turquoise— generally set in a ring which had to be worn on the index or little finger for its spell to be potent—whenever they travelled, in the same way that Western men wear a St. Christopher medal. Persian women wore small 'seed' turquoises as a charm against sterility.

The turquoise, as its name suggests, came originally from the Middle East, the earliest known mines being in the Sinai peninsula and in Persia. It was brought through Turkey, being given the name *pierre turquoise* on its way to Europe, where it was used in the jewellery of famous queens and princesses in many of the Western countries. The earliest dated piece is said to be an Egyptian bracelet set with turquoises which probably came from the Sinai peninsula mines.

It is claimed that it was the ancient Venetians who gave the gem its name, which means Turkesa or Turkey Stone, and was formerly spelled turkois. However it happened, it has through the centuries come to be called turquoise and by that name it is known throughout the world today.

Like many other precious stones and gemstones it is composed mainly of aluminium, but it is unique otherwise in that it is the only one that belongs to the phosphates. It is a hydrous phosphate of aluminium with a small percentage of copper and iron oxides —the former giving the stone its blue colouring.

Actually 'blue' is a loose way of describing the colour of the turquoise, for it ranges in colour from sky-blue to an aqueous green containing both blue and green tones. The really intense blue is but rarely seen and is, naturally enough, the colour most prized in both Europe and the East. As the blue descends in tone to green so its value deteriorates until it becomes entirely green in which colour it is used only in some parts of Arabia for inferior jewels.

Since the most important mines today are in Mexico, formerly the Aztec kingdom, it is natural that the stone should have been much prized by the ancient Mexicans, who valued it far above gold. At that time it was the green stone which was the more highly esteemed.

So far as the United States is concerned most of the turquoises come from the New Mexico mines, but they are also found in California, Colorado and Arizona. The most important mines for the finer gems are in Asia, especially Persia, whose products are regarded as the highest quality of stones. Some of these mines have been worked for centuries and are mentioned by the Arab Mohammed-ibn-Mansu in his treatise written in A.D. 1300.

Turquoises are freely found in the districts round the Sinai peninsula, where the best-known mines are situated in the Wadi

Moghara or Hollow Valley. These are very ancient and were worked on a large scale in ancient Egyptian times, as early, in fact, as the Third Dynasty, 4000 B.C. The mines were regarded as so important that the ancient Egyptians maintained a garrison there to protect them.

The turquoise is also found in porphyry, outside the Wadi Moghara, which it penetrates in thin plates so that the beautiful blue colour is permanent. Other mines are situated at the site of the Well of Moses, Nesch, and the Nasaiph Well between Suez and Sinai. The best stones from the latter mines are equal to Persian stones and even sometimes surpass them in beauty and depth of colouring. Fine stones from this locality are sold as Egyptian and Alexandrian turquoises.

The price of turquoises varies according to size and colour, although large ones are not sold in proportion to their weight because of their rarity. The largest and finest turquoise in existence is believed to be one that is in the treasury of the Shah of Persia.

Most of the blue stones have a tendency to turn greenish with age as they absorb grease and oil or lose water, and numerous fraudulent attempts have been made to try to restore the colour that has faded. Other attempts have been made to improve the colour of turquoises, but only a few have met with any sort of success. Form certain localities, of course, the true colour of the gem is constant.

Turquoise has a waxy lustre which serves to conceal scratches, which is fortunate, for the gem is not particularly hard and is easily marked. Glass imitations, which are not uncommon, show small bubbles under the surface, while imitations, of enamel and stained chalcedony, show none of the typical veining which characterizes the true turquoise. Odontolite or 'bone turquoise', a fossil ivory of bone which has become stained blue by the iron phosphate mineral vivianite, is a natural mineral resembling turquoise and has often appeared as a substitute for it. Amazonite (a feldspar) may also be mistaken for turquoise of poor quality, but its lower density and refractive index will distinguish it.

Cheap turquoise is often waxed in an attempt to disguise its poor quality of polish.

Usually turquoise is cut as an ornamental stone in circular or elliptical form and generally has a low convex surface. Gemstones of curious shape and bright colouring were highly esteemed in the days before it was thought worth while to cut and polish stones, and little regard was paid to the transparent gems now so highly prized. The turquoise still holds a prominent place in Occidental jewellery.

Zircons, which come from Siam and Ceylon, of the colourless or white variety, are the nearest approach in appearance and brilliance to a real diamond. The zircon has a high refractivity of light and lends itself well to the cutting and faceting used in diamond cutting. Naturally a golden-brown stone, it has been transmuted by heat treatment to a clear and pretty blue shade. An increase in the heat treatment is used to make the zircon white or colourless, and in this form it is often bought as a substitute for a diamond where a large stone is desired and the price of a diamond of a similar size would be prohibitive. So long as an effect of a diamond without regard to its intrinsic value is sufficient, then the white zircon is about the best substitute. Other colours of zircons include yellow, orange, red and sherry brown, and in these shades the stone is called a hyacinth. Zircons of Victorian days were sometimes described as 'jargoons'. Quite often the zircon in its different shades is sold under rather misleading names such as 'Siam aquamarine' (the blue variety) or 'Ceylon diamond' (the colourless zircon). A simple gemmological test will soon resolve any doubts on the matter, apart from the obvious fact that a zircon could not long deceive because of its inferior hardness.

CHAPTER THREE

Rings

RINGS, perhaps more than any other form of jewellery, are the most universally worn jewels. If a census were to be taken of those who own only one piece of jewellery it is probable that in ninety cases out of a hundred it would be found to be a ring. Not only because the giving of a ring is an important concomitant of a betrothal, but also because of its significance in official as well as in private affairs.

From the time of the Pharaohs rings were worn as talismans and amulets. In the days when poisoning was a favoured method of disposing of unpopular people, rings were worn that were believed to have the virtue of being able to betray the presence of undesirable 'foreign matter' in food and drink. Excavations of famous tombs have yielded up examples of these particular 'poison-detecting' rings still on the fingers of the mummies. It was also believed that all the dangers of travel and sudden death were averted by wearing rings adorned with cabalistic signs. In medieval times rings inscribed with the names of the Three Magi were regarded as a powerful charm against any disaster; when set with rubies they were further believed to have the power of giving warning against impending danger. In the Middle Ages rings of silver set with a round piece of muddy coloured bone were worn by women and children as a protection against evil during the absence of the men of the household. These rings were supposed to change colour if the wearer was poisoned, or taken seriously ill so that remedial steps could be taken in time, leading to the stones being called 'givers of life'.

In the days when the art of writing was known only to a privileged few it was the custom for men to wear a ring on which some distinguishing sign or badge was engraved, so that by using it as a seal it would give authority and authenticity to letters and documents. When a royal person desired to delegate his authority to an official he would hand to that person a signet ring, so giving him the full royal authority in his commands.

Some of the earliest existing rings date from about the Eighteenth to the Twentieth Dynasties. These are of pure gold, crude and massive, with the name and title of the owner in hieroglyphics on an oblong gold 'table' (the enlarged part of the ring on which the design is engraved or a stone set is called the 'table', and the circlet and so on the 'shank'). Not all these early rings, however, were of pure gold; some were of silver, bronze, glass or pottery, the latter material being covered with a siliceous glaze in brilliant blues and greens coloured by means of copper oxides. Some were made of ivory, amber and cornelian—all hard stones. In the Twelfth and subsequent Dynasties of Egypt the scarab was very popular as an amulet, formed or engraved on the table of the rings of the period. Phoenician rings also carried a scarab or some other amulet, but in their case usually in a box setting on a swivel claw, to be used for sealing purposes and then swivelled inwards. A gold swivel ring mounted with a scarab was very largely used by the Etruscans, though another and more plentiful class of signet rings had scarabs cut in sard or cornelian, cut on the 'table' in the Hellenic style, with the scarab beetle carved underneath. All were very large and elaborate.

Iron rings were worn by the majority of citizens of the Roman Republic. Ambassadors were the first to be privileged to wear gold rings and then only when they were performing some public duty. Then the right to wear rings was extended to senators, consuls, equites (or knights) and all the chief officials of state. Throughout the Roman Empire there were many different laws relating to the wearing of rings. For instance, Tiberius made a large property qualification necessary for the wearing of gold rings by those who were not of 'free' descent, while Severus conceded the right to all Roman soldiers—later on to all free citizens. Silver rings were worn by freedmen and iron rings by slaves, but even these restrictions passed away under Justinian. At this time ring decoration was not confined to the 'table' alone but was used on the shank, often polygonal or angular. Those Roman rings of the third and fourth centuries A.D. were engraved with Christian symbols; some with the monogram of Christ and some with a dove within an olive wreath.

Early Celts made their rings—often of penannular form—of the purest gold (penannular meaning having a break in the complete circle, often to form a spring). These usually consisted of a simple bar of gold twisted in an ornamental way, or gold wire twisted into a rope design, often used in place of money. Throughout the Middle Ages the ring continued to be an article of importance in religious, legal, commercial and private life.

There seems to be little doubt that the episcopal ring, solemnly conferred upon a newly made bishop, derived from the signet ring and its assumption of authority. The first mention of the episcopal ring was made in a decree of Pope Boniface IV at Rome in A.D. 610 and a special formula for the solemn conferment on the newly made bishop was inserted in the Pontifical. Sometimes an antique gem was set in the bishop's ring and an inscription added in the gold setting. More commonly the episcopal ring was set with a large amethyst, ruby, sapphire or other stone cut *en cabochon* and very magnificent in effect. The amethyst, known in earlier times as the 'stone of authority' was for this reason most often chosen. Because the pontifical ring used at Mass was worn over the bishop's glove, it was (and still is) of a massive size. The 'Papal Ring of the Fisherman' is described as bearing the device of St Peter in a boat drawing a net through the water, representing the 'fisher of men'. After the death of a Pope the Papal Ring is broken and a new ring with a space for the name left blank is taken into the Conclave and placed on the finger of the newly elected Pontiff, who then declares what name he will assume and gives the ring back to be engraved with the name he has chosen.

The custom of giving a ring to mark a betrothal is believed to be of Roman origin. Originally the custom was for a plain ring of iron to be used, the gold ring being introduced in the second century. Of secular origin, it later received ecclesiastical sanction and formulae for the benediction of the ring exist from the eleventh century.

Gemmel or gimmel rings, from the Latin *gemellus*, a twin, made with two 'shanks' fitted together which could be worn either together or singly, were in common use in the sixteenth and seventeenth centuries as betrothal rings. At this time, too, posy rings—so-called from the poesy or rhyme engraved upon them—were very popular. At this time wedding rings were also engraved with poesies, such as 'Love and obaye', 'Fear God and love me'. The seventeenth century also saw the introduction of memorial rings in various mournful forms, usually enamelled in black and white, carrying a name and date of death. Some of the more extreme of these were coffin shaped, or in the form of two skeletons making the shank, with a coffin as the 'table'. It was common practice for a specified sum of money to be left by will for the buying of mourning rings for distribution among friends and family.

Other interesting rings of earlier times included the 'cramp' rings which were much worn in the Middle Ages as a protection against cramp—their virtue arising from their having been blessed by the king in a special form of service for the purpose. Decade rings were another fancy in the fifteenth century, used after the manner of rosaries to recite nine Aves and a Paternoster. Thumb rings, worn from the fourteenth to the seventeenth century, are referred to by Shakespeare when he makes Falstaff boast of having been slender enough in his youth to be able to 'creep into any alderman's thumb ring'.

During the eighteenth and nineteenth centuries both engagement and wedding rings were usually of heavy gold; gems were of less importance than the precious metal. 'Gipsy' rings were favoured by both men and women and were very popular as engagement rings. Rather an unaesthetic fashion, these gipsy rings consisted of a broad, D-shaped band of gold into which one or three diamonds were so deeply sunk as to be almost flush with the metal. Star incisions in the metal round the gems were made to give the effect of rays going out from the stones.

While most women favoured the gipsy ring set with three diamonds, men usually wore the one-diamond style.

At this period, too, the 'keeper' ring became fashionable. This was a very wide band of gold deeply engraved with an all-over design which was worn above the wedding ring, hence the name 'keeper' ring. Some of these were deeply incised with the word 'Mizpah', which was said to mean 'The Lord be between thee and me when we are absent one from the other'. Sometimes the word, instead of being engraved, was deeply carved into the gold so that it stood out in relief from the gold band. Gold and silver brooches of this period also bore the word 'Mizpah' and were a favourite family gift, especially to a new baby.

With the twentieth century the seven-stone diamond cluster, or a central coloured gem surrounded by diamonds, were high fashion for engagement rings, while for wedding rings the D-shaped plain gold band (but a more flattened D-shape than that of today) reigned supreme and continued until well into the 1930's. Just before the Second World War changes in design began to appear. The ring itself became narrower and platinum made its appearance in wedding rings, probably with the idea, originally, of matching the platinum setting which was now being used for setting diamonds in engagement rings. In Britain with the outbreak of war and the cessation of a free supply of gold, government controls brought into being the narrow gold wedding ring of only nine carats. These 'Government' rings sold at just under thirty shillings each, price controlled. Once gold began to trickle back into circulation in the later post-war years designers began to give freer rein to their imagination and produced a wide diversity of styles. Two-colour rings used white and yellow gold to make a pattern; platinum became more and more popular in octagonal shapes, each section in turn plain and patterned; facetings in both gold and platinum were all fashions of the post-war years, while the wedding ring grew narrower and narrower in size.

Today broader rings are returning to favour again, some very elaborately decorated with chased or pierced work. Open-work designs are strikingly featured in gold rings composed of open chain links engraved and with finely granulated edges. This form of decoration, popular in early Phoenician times, is making a reappearance in modern gold jewellery, especially rings. There are, too, linked chain wedding rings in which platinum links alternate with gold ones. Flower posies of hand-carved gold make another outstanding modern style on the lines of the Victorian keeper ring. Yet another modern design is reminiscent of the Prince of Wales's crown in that it has carved gold representations of jewels all around the ring, similar in size and shape to the diamond-set eternity ring. All the designs are hand-carved—a process which results in greater depth in the pattern. Many women owning less fashionable, plain gold wedding rings are having them modernized to follow this trend for patterning. As long as the gold of the original wedding ring is used for making the new design, sentiment is satisfied and the owners are apparently content to have their old wedding ring melted down for the modernizing process.

Eternity rings—rings in which the gems are set right around the circlet—first came into vogue in the 'thirties and are usually given as anniversary gifts today, though they are sometimes chosen as wedding rings. The favourite design is eight-sided, each section either entirely diamond set, or alternately set with rubies and diamonds, emeralds and diamonds, or sapphires and diamonds. Swivel eternity rings consist of a complete hoop set in diamonds and two half-hoops, one of sapphires and the other of rubies, which are hinged at each side of the ring. These can then be switched at will. All three can be worn to show at the same time, or the diamonds can be seen with either the rubies or the sapphires as a two-colour instead of a three-colour ring.

CHAPTER FOUR

The bracelet

LIKE most jewellery, the earliest examples of the bracelet worn as a personal adornment as well as a sign of rank are to be found in the archives of ancient Egypt. From the earliest periods, the ancient kings' jewellers made jewels which as well as being decorative were intended to indicate the rank and status of the wearers. Even before jewellers translated the fashion into terms of precious metals and gems bracelets were indicated by painted bands round the arms, for sculpture and paintings of earliest Egyptians show bands of red and blue colour on the arms, both above and below the elbow.

Some of the earliest examples of actual bracelets were composed of glass and gold beads, with others of solid gold, quite plain except for a border of chain work. Bracelets of the Twelfth Dynasty were of thick and thin gold wire, usually with beaten-out ends which were twisted one over the other to form a method of fastening. Others in the shape of gold serpents (still in fashion) were worn in the Ptolemaic and early Roman periods.

The classically beautiful arms of the women of Ancient Greece (if we are to believe the evidence of remaining statuary) must have been a great inspiration to the goldsmiths of the period. Certainly the workmanship from the close of the fifth century onwards was of impressive fineness, though there was, perhaps, little diversity in design. Bracelets and armlets chiefly followed three basic styles—a fine plaited chain with a clasp in the form of a knot; plaques adorned with repoussé work, hinged together for flexibility; and a plain circular band of beaten gold.

Amber was used in abundance by the Etruscan jewellers who also showed great skill in the use of granulation, exemplified by many pieces in the Metropolitan Museum of Art, New York. Bracelets were a favourite form of jewel with the early Romans, though like the ancient Greeks, little variation of design was shown and the bracelets of the period were chiefly made in two forms, one intended to be worn wound round the wrist and fashioned on the same lines as the necklaces of the period; the other of two halves of solid gold, hinged, and closed by a snap. The second kind of bracelet was worn on the upper arm and though originally made of pure gold, jewellers later set them with precious stones. A fine pair of bracelets of the period is to be seen in the Metropolitan Museum of Art, the open ends of each bracelet terminating in beautifully modelled rams' heads.

Byzantine jewellery was always renowned for its lavishness and bracelets were prominent among the extravaganza of jewels of the time, characterized by intricacy of design and richness of gems. An indication of the diversity of fine detail which went to their making is shown in a bracelet in the Franks bequest (donated to the British nation by Sir Augustus Wollaston Franks (1826–1897), the noted English authority on mediaeval antiquities) which is in the form of a pointwork hoop decorated with swans and bouquets enclosed in scrolls issuing from an urn. Even the clasp is decorated, being composed of a medallion adorned with a bust of the Virgin in repoussé work. The Empress Theodora is portrayed wearing eight bracelets on each arm, while her Court ladies had glittering bracelets reaching from wrist to elbow.

Men and women of the Romano-British period wore gold ornaments for the arms which were known as *armillae*, usually very plain, though some were twisted in broad and narrow designs. Those that have survived, however, are mostly of bronze following the same designs as those of gold. The fastenings were in the form of tapering ends placed one over the other, or of a simple hook and eye. Circlets of vivid blue transparent glass—a hint of the slave bangles of the second decade of the twentieth century A.D.—were also worn at this period.

The Anglo-Saxon age saw the goldsmiths increase in stature and importance. The majority of the monks of the time were skilled goldsmiths who did not confine their work entirely to ecclesiastical pieces. Then, too, the jewellery of the time was famous for its delicacy of workmanship and blending of colours in the beautiful enamelling with which it was characterized. This is particularly true of the Anglo-Saxon jewellery of the seventh and ninth centuries in which much cloisonné enamel work was prominent. The Venerable Bede was moved to write with enthusiasm of the craft of the time and the excellence of the monk-goldsmiths' work.

Medieval times saw an increase in the amount of jewellery worn, and the reign of Edward III was literally rendered brilliant by reason of the jewels to be seen everywhere. And the fashion for personal jewellery or *bravouries* increased still more during the reign of Richard II, though bracelets were not so much in vogue during the Middle Ages. The ladies of that time confined themselves to wearing rosaries and chaplets of beads wound round their wrists. Many paintings of the time show what might be taken for jewelled bracelets round the upper arm, over the long and extravagant sleeves, but it is more likely that these were bands of material, richly gold-embroidered and gem-set, which were sewn on to the sleeves.

Armlets and bracelets were certainly worn in the fifteenth century but generally only during the summer. Fashions of the Renaissance did little, in fact, to help the display of bracelets and even to some extent discouraged the fashion. Sleeves were worn long and full, falling gracefully over the hands, and since bracelets, if worn, could not be seen, they retreated as a fashion. Some women, however, were not to be defeated and continued to wear bracelets, chiefly composed of beads of amber or agate, separated by balls of gold, over the sleeves, whilst others had their sleeves slashed to reveal the bracelets beneath. Men as well as women followed the fashion for bracelets, as an inventory made of Henry VIII's in 1530 shows. This mentions no fewer than seventeen, including one of 'Paris work with jacynths' and one with 'eight diamonds, eight rubies, fourteen pearls and a diamond rose'. Mary Stuart also possessed many beautiful bracelets, including one of filigree pendants enclosing scent, a charming fashion of the time and one which might well be revived.

Though they never really completely disappeared, bracelets

seem, so far as historical records show, to have skipped a few centuries. Perhaps the long sleeves already referred to were largely responsible for when sleeve fashions changed about the eighteenth century and they began to be worn above or at elbow length the bracelet immediately returned as a favourite jewel. With bare forearms, what more natural than to decorate them with two or even four or five bracelets? Sometimes the bracelets were worn simply; quite frequently they consisted of several rows of gems joined together—particularly of pearls. At this time there was, too, a simplified form of bracelet, French in inspiration, which consisted of a ribbon band to which was attached a jewelled motif, usually a brooch. It was a pretty fashion but it did not, apparently, satisfy entirely the need for decorative jewellery, for the bracelet of linked cameos next appeared, owing its influence to the Directoire period. Where hitherto bracelets had followed the classical form of rigid, wide bands of metal, they now became flexible, generally with a handsomely jewelled central ornament with links going from each side to the clasp.

The Empire period saw an increase in the wearing of the bracelet which became accordingly more and more elaborate and diverse. Those of French workmanship followed the fashion in other personal jewellery and generally matched necklaces, intricate settings and a lavish use of precious gems were characteristic. Gemstones, too, were popular at this time, and the more massive types of bracelet were set with agates, moonstones, cat's-eyes and similar stones. Turquoises set around with small brilliants and joined by fine gold links were frequently seen. The Empress Josephine extended her passion for cameos to bracelets composed of these 'medallions' linked by diamonds. Later, women of fashion wore velvet ribbon bracelets with a central cameo, a fashion which was revived in mid-Victorian days.

It was during the early part of the nineteenth century that the links which had appeared earlier developed into the expanding bracelet which could be slipped over the hand without fastening or clasp. This was achieved by a series of springs at the links and was rightly considered a notable step forward in jewellery craftsmanship. Though this form of bracelet remained in favour there was at the same time a return to the rigid, wide band of gold or silver, richly engraved with mythological figures or with flowers and foliage.

All were hand-made and for some time both solid and linked flexible bracelets were worn. The advent of the machine age in the second half of the nineteenth century stepped up the production of bracelets of all kinds. Except where the bracelet was part of a parure of precious gems they usually were composed simply of a precious metal, the adornment taking the form of engraving, chasing and applied work. Very wide bracelets, hinged and with snap fastenings, were engraved with an all-over design rather like the keeper rings of the period. But there were, too, rigid bangles richly chased and set with diamonds at intervals. These were not hinged, but were slipped over the hand and were either round or oval in shape. Heavy 'curb' bracelets of simple links, finished off with a locket in the form of a heart padlock (often complete with tiny gold key), usually in 9 carat gold, were fashionable. There were also at this time bracelets made of elephant's hair, which were supposed to have the virtue of being luck-bringers.

Coming to the twentieth-century version of the bracelet fashion the first decade saw the stiff bracelet in high favour. These might be of ring or oval shape, in gold set with diamonds and other precious stones, or with the stones set in a simple row on the upper half of the bracelet only. Or the gold might be in the form of a separated double row, hinged, with a half-hoop of diamonds or coloured gems set between the two rows. Strictly speaking, these were bangles rather than bracelets, the latter term being used today to describe a flexible circlet. Along with Edward VII's reign came faceted gold bracelets and flat-surfaced ones decorated with engine-turning, while the bracelet in the form of a serpent was still worn—a fashion which has persisted through several thousand years, hard as that may be to believe.

As the present century progressed into the 'twenties and the 'thirties the 'slave bangle' worn on the upper arm was in vogue.

These were contemporary with the Charleston and the Black Bottom, and the fashion was to wear an extravagantly long chiffon handkerchief of vivid colour threaded through the slave bangle. Penannular bracelets—a broken circle—were also in fashion, with the heads of the break flattened out into fancy shapes. Others were gem-set at the break and these two decorative gem-set ends were made detachable to form dress clips. Hinged wide-band bracelets had a large medallion decoration set with gemstones such as topaz, amethyst, turquoise, and so on, and with half-pearls. Some of these were very wide, set in a rococo fashion of richness.

More and more diamond-set bracelets began to appear as the present century advanced, and with them the greatest variety of designs of any other form of jewellery. The main theme for flexible gem-set bracelets was for recurrent motifs linked by diamonds and using rubies, emeralds, and sapphires to achieve colour. At the same time these trends have widened and developed to embrace endless permutations of precious gem-setting. In the field of bracelets made entirely of precious metal the contemporary craftsman is producing miracles of engineering skill in weaving fine gold wire into a fabric-like mesh to make bracelets of great decorative quality and flexibility. This weaving is varied from the plain warp and weft to intricate patterns of diamonds, squares and zig-zag weaves. Most of these are either spattered with diamonds and other gems or have an elaborate jewelled motif which can be removed at will and worn as a dress clip. Ingenuity and variety may truly be said to be the twin qualities of twentieth-century bracelets.

Modern designers have done much to keep alive a delightfully decorative fashion, and the bracelets of today are distinguished both by versatility of design and beauty. Skilled workmanship has evolved a flexibility of setting which gives a ribbon-like suppleness to even the most heavily gem-set bracelets, so that both precious stones and metals have an added beauty, and impart even greater charm and grace to a well-shaped wrist.

CHAPTER FIVE

The necklace

THROUGHOUT the history of mankind's evolution from the Palaeolithic Age to the present day one jewel which has constantly recurred is the necklace. Crudely wrought, but showing the earliest desire for adornment, necklaces have been found buried with the remains of the prehistoric dead. The Egyptians, highly civilized at a time when the people of Western Europe were living like troglodytes lurking in the blackness of caves, were wearing exquisite necklaces of fine workmanship which have since been found sealed up in their tombs. The sepulchres of ancient Mycenae, the sarcophagi of ancient Crete, the excavations on the other Greek islands and in Etruria—all have in their time yielded an abundance of necklaces among the jewels unearthed by the archaeologists. It would seem that the necklace was indeed one of the very earliest forms of personal decoration, the very genus of jewellery even if these earlier forms were simply shells or stone beads strung together by primitive peoples.

It seems hard to believe that an amazing delicacy of workmanship characterized Egyptian necklaces of cornelian, gold, amethyst and jasper dating from 2000 B.C. As long ago as the Eighteenth Dynasty (1400 B.C.) the Egyptians devised necklaces of polychrome faience from which hung pendants in the form of flowers. And even 3,000 years before that they had developed amazing skill in the application of coloured glazes to beads for necklaces. Some were in the form of a series of star-like flowers suspended from a fine gold chain; others showed the inlaying of coloured gems which seems to have been a feature of the jewellery of the period, sure in intention, elegant in workmanship and completely decorative.

Insects and scarabs abounded as decoration for ancient Egyptian necklace adornments, sometimes forming pendant drops from the circlet, sometimes forming the clasp to a plain circlet of gold. The jeweller-craftsmen of those thousands of years ago made the natural form of animals serve a functional purpose expressed in the case of the necklace of a queen of the Eighteenth Dynasty which had a fastening made of the heads of water fowl, their gracefully arched necks forming loops to hook one into the other. The necklace itself is of gold wire so finely plaited that it achieves complete flexibility, with a quaint scarab of gold inlaid with lapis lazuli hanging from the front by a small gold ring.

Some of the finest examples of early Greek necklaces, adorned with gold rosettes set with coloured stones and other fancies, were often used as barter. In this way Greek jewellery found its way to the Black Sea coast, the merchants in Athens having exported the necklaces and other jewellery to the distant settlements colonized by the Greeks to be given in exchange for fish and wheat.

The luxuriousness of life in ancient Rome is reflected in the jewellery of the time, when women of high rank wore necklaces richly set with coloured stones, though gold was the predominant medium for making most of the jewels of that time and place. Necklaces were chiefly composed of gold chains of varying patterns and designs from which hung gold coins, medallions, rosettes and other pendant fancies. But the decline in civilization was marked, as almost invariably happens, by a simultaneous decline in the arts, and the decay of the Roman Empire is as clearly traceable from remaining examples of jewellery as from any written history, as a study of the contemporary jewels in the principal museums will show. Then, too, the influx of the barbarian tribes and the development of the Teutonic style saw a debasement of classical art. Necklaces of the period clearly show the retrogression which succeeded the purity of the classical style. In necklaces it was betrayed in a heavier, clumsier style; instead of the delicacy of the plaited gold wire and chain, necklaces displayed rather crude bird and beast forms cut from stones and set in heavy, perforated gold plate. Where before Roman women had necklaces of small massed stones, more massive styles, containing more and larger gems, became the vogue.

Choker necklaces were in fashion in the fifth century, when Merovingian jewellery included choker necklaces composed of slabs of garnet set into thin plates of gold, looking like cloisonné enamel. Other choker necklaces, i.e. those worn circling closely the base of the throat, were in gold filigree work of great delicacy.

As period merged into period necklaces varied in form and material. In Saxon England King Alfred was personally interesting himself in the jeweller's craft, and the skill of the lapidaries, under such royal encouragement, had progressed sufficiently to enable them to pierce stones with some degree of precision, thus widening the scope for design. Necklaces of amber and amethysts were now worn, although amber beads had, of course, been used as neck ornaments from the earliest times.

At the close of the thirteenth century jewellery became more and more popular, stimulated by the Crusading knights who returned laden with the spoils of war which included rich gemstones for their delighted womenfolk. Their ingenuity in putting this rich booty to the adornment of their clothes and persons eventually led, in Britain, to Parliament's enacting sumptuary laws in 1363 regulating and restricting the extravagant use of personal adornment. Whether by design or intention, the fashions conspired to support the King's desire for less ostentation, for in the thirteenth and fourteenth centuries, throughout Europe the wimple came into vogue and completely hid the neck. The necklace was therefore out. But not for long. The wimple went the way of all fashions, and necklaces returned to favour, with greater richness and diversity than ever.

Throughout Europe necklaces were still being worn; jewels of elaborate richness but depending more on gold than on gems. Among those of the fourteenth century to be seen in the Hispano-Moresque jewels in the Metropolitan Museum of Art, there are necklaces which show the use of repoussé, engraved and granulated gold, often combined with cloisonné enamel. The necklace itself usually consisted of linked flat circular gold discs with pendant motifs of gold or cloisonné enamel set at regular intervals at the front.

Necklaces of the Renaissance period were notable chiefly for their handsome pendants, in the making of which German and

Italian jewellers were pre-eminent. Many were of grotesque character, determined by the odd shape of a central baroque pearl around which the design was built. Typical examples in the Metropolitan Museum of Art include an enamelled gold swan with baroque pearl centre, hanging from gold links set with pearls, believed to be sixteenth century Italian. The pendant of another necklace of this period is in the form of a monkey in enamelled gold and rubies with a single drop pearl below, of the latter half of the sixteenth century and of German origin.

While Byzantine women had for centuries followed the fashion for wearing necklaces—often as many as ten at a time ranging in length from short chokers fitting to the base of the throat, to knee-length—it was not until the fifteenth century that necklaces of precious stones were worn in Western Europe. The fashion for these is believed to have originated in France in the time of the French King Charles VII, though contemporary paintings by the great Italian masters show women wearing handsome necklaces of pearls with jewelled pendants. Many of the foremost painters of the fifteenth and sixteenth centuries were trained as goldsmiths —Botticelli, Ghirlandajo, Dürer, Holbein, to name but a few. Ghirlandajo in fact owed his name to the necklaces fashioned by his 'master' goldsmith for the ladies of Florence, Ghirlandajo being a nickname derived from these jewelled garlands. Holbein's necklaces of the fifteenth and sixteenth centuries were designed chiefly for men. Dress fashions then, as now, influenced jewel fashions. In the sixteenth century men had abandoned their long cloaks and dalmaticas and were wearing short doublets, cut very full to achieve a squared silhouette, with sleeves of exaggerated width. Women wore the same huge sleeves, with tight waists and skirts billowing to floor length. Both wore jewelled chain necklaces, strings of pearls and some fine pendants. Although in Italy costume was being modified in both style and colour and the use of jewellery was heavily restrained, in other parts of Europe (except Britain) no curb was placed on personal adornment and both men and women wore heavily gemmed necklaces with handsome pendants.

When the fifteenth century brought in the shoulder-revealing décolleté the necklace gained even greater importance and grandeur. In addition to a choker necklet of large precious stones, another longer and equally handsome necklace was worn with it. Often a third necklace was added to the other two, though this usually took the form of a simple chain of gold carrying, however, a magnificently jewelled pendant. Men's and women's necklaces did not differ greatly in character and it was not uncommon for mothers to lend their necklaces to their sons for an occasion.

When the first Elizabethan era arrived it was soon to be seen that the daughter of Henry VIII had inherited her father's love of jewels, though through her life her favourite gem was the pearl. She was, however, an ambassadress for the products of the empire she controlled and she deemed it her royal duty to wear the gems which were coming across the sea. But her predilection for pearls for a time almost led to the exclusion of other precious gems from fashion. She would wear four, five, six or more necklaces of ropes of pearls, the longest extending to her knees. One wonders where these priceless gems are today.

In the seventeenth century more thought and craftsmanship began to be given to the setting of precious gems, hitherto more conspicuous for size than for artistry. Diamonds were set in silver; coloured gems in gold. Designs of flowers, wreaths, leaves and ribband knots were used extensively and with great effect. It was unfortunate that the British Civil War of the seventeenth century called upon the people to sacrifice their jewels to financing the struggle and, for that period the craft lay more or less dormant. But the dawn of the eighteenth century saw a resurgence of social life and of fashion and though French jewellers were dominating the scene, the British jewellery craft—as good, if not better—moved forward. The Rococo was in strong favour, and intricate designs of flowers, ribbons, scrolls and leaves characterized necklaces of the early period though these designs did not long remain in favour. The influence of Madame de Pompadour began to be felt and expressed itself in lighter and more graceful jewellery, the high-dressed Pompadour coiffure focusing interest on the necklace. There was a renaissance of coloured gold, and portrait necklaces—consisting of a series of miniature portraits, each surrounded by diamond brilliants, joined together by diamond links—were worn. A favourite sequence was that showing a girl from babyhood to womanhood.

Low necklines prevailed in the early nineteenth century and the Empire period, following the lines of the shoulders with a shallow scoop in front. These naturally gave great scope for wearing in profusion important diamond necklaces of great splendour. Colour was the keynote and necklaces of delicate goldwork were frequently set with pink and golden topaz, small turquoises and half-pearls, further embellished by a somewhat large drop pendant echoing the stones of the necklace itself.

As the nineteenth century progressed the necklace grew still more important. The early Victorian bouffant crinoline gown, with its off-the-shoulder neckline, created a demand for important necklaces to decorate the low décolletage and the parure of precious gems became popular. This usually consisted of a large corsage brooch in the form of a flower spray with foliage, usually diamond-set, or scrolls and bars in an intricate design; a handsome necklace, ear-rings (generally of the long, drop kind) and a tiara. Diamonds and other precious gems were so massed in these suites that women to whom they were handed down as heirlooms used them for remodelling into more modern designs. It is a pity, for the present vogue for Victoriana would have made them, in their original form, so much more intriguing.

Mid-Victorian days and later the *fin de siècle* period brought about a heaviness of fashion which was reflected in the jewellery of the time. During the day it was somewhat sombre; at night it was rich and plentiful, with the necklace very much in evidence. Once again chain necklaces came into vogue, but now interspersed with garnets, amethysts, topaz, pearls and other gemstones. They were rather long and were worn looped once or twice around the neck and caught up on the left breast, secured in place with a large cameo, a brooch of twisted and decorated gold, or a Florentine inlay brooch.

With the death of the Prince Consort and the fashion for sombre mourning jewellery the jet necklace came to the forefront. Faceted or carved, it ranged from a single row of 'beads' to a triple row of diamond-shaped jet, or a fringe of jet drops hanging from a single-row necklace. In more sombre style a thick black silk cord would be used to suspend a carved 'In Memoriam' pendant. All this was in curious contrast with the material opulence of the middle and upper classes.

All this ended with the accession of King Edward VII in the first year of the twentieth century and the opening of the Edwardian age. The King was gay and loved to see pretty women prettily decked. His fair Queen Alexandra with her diamond 'dog-collar necklaces brought into fashion the diamond collet necklace with pendeloque diamonds. Her favourite style, however, was the triple row of diamonds worn closely round the base of the throat. Women who did not aspire to diamonds satisfied themselves with necklaces set with garnets, olivines, amethysts and moonstones. In contrast there was a fashion for thin gold chain necklaces with a pendant set with either these stones or aquamarines, light and delicate enough for daytime wear.

With the 'twenties came the 'flapper', the Charleston and Black Bottom, Adèle and Fred Astaire—and bead necklaces. These were of singularly unimaginative design, just ropes of beads of all sorts and sizes, hanging sometimes to the knees so that they would sway about like Maypole ribbons as their wearers cavorted in the Charleston, the heavily fringed, knee-length dresses of the day swinging out in unison with the beads. It was a frustrating time for the jewellery designer and lasted well into the 'thirties. That decade produced necklaces of what is known as 'matinée' length—about six inches long from the centre front. Those set with precious gems were two rather than three dimensional; there were many chain necklaces again, but now the links were more ornamental and interspersed with crystals and coloured beads alternating. Fine gold chains with heart and book-shaped lockets were worn, vying for popularity with flexible gold 'Brazilian-woven' chokers. Necklaces for formal occasions used clusters of precious gems, shaped like the gold torque of the early Celts, and beginning to show indications of the sculptured line that was to come later.

In the period since the end of the Second World War jewellery designs have made immense strides forward and the most notable developments have been in the design of necklaces. Today the diversity of design, of form, of colour and of setting is exciting and ranks the jeweller's craft with that of the sculptor or painter. Once again precious gems are massed, but instead of a conglomeration of stones there is a highly artistic form style; pavé-set diamonds and other gems are used for a gracefully curving background to central motifs. It is recognized that the appeal of a jewel is greater if a large piece of jewellery can be utilized on other, less formal occasions. In this field modern jewellery designers have exercised great ingenuity in necklaces, some of which are capable of dismantling to form four, five or even six different jewels. This calls for the highest skill in design and craftsmanship which is seen at its best where an apparently single-purpose necklace can be transformed into a bracelet, a pair of earclips and a dress clip. In choosing necklaces to harmonize with the fashions of the moment the designer is influenced by the unusual colour schemes provided by the lesser-known gemstones. As well as the ever-impressive diamond, modern necklaces use such unusual and contrasting stones as peridot and pearls, turquoise and pearls. The navy blue of sapphire is allied to the green of the emerald; the red of a perfect ruby is daringly contrasted with topaz or with the blue of aquamarine. Closely woven fine gold wire forms a 'cloth of gold' which, spattered with tiny diamonds, emeralds, rubies and sapphires, is made into enchanting necklaces which have matching earclips, dress clip and bracelet. Sometimes coarser gold wire of more rigid quality is used to make latticed necklaces, or fronded ones like the waving fronds of the sea anemone. Truly it is an age of variety, imagination and creativeness, never better expressed by the jeweller than in the creation of necklaces.

CHAPTER SIX

The ear-ring

OF all items of jewellery in the nineteen-sixties perhaps the most universally popular is the ear-ring. Women collect ear-rings as assiduously as children search for brightly coloured shells on the seashore, and it is nothing to learn of girls who have collections numbering a hundred different pairs. Men look on this passion for ear-rings with an indulgent or—depending on temperament and perhaps age—a deprecating eye. Yet ear-rings were once a masculine fashion, for history records the wearing of ear-rings by men in very ancient times, and cites the examples taken from the tombs of Ur of the Chaldees which date from 3500 B.C.

Sir Walter Raleigh, representative of the Court gallants of the Renaissance, wore pearl ear-rings, as did many of his fashionable contemporaries. Shakespeare and other actors at the Globe Theatre also wore them. The wearing of twin pearls as a single ear-ring, usually on the left ear, was especially distinctive of the Elizabethan period.

The history of the ear-ring goes back to Biblical times, and many references are made to them in the Old Testament. Some of the ancient Etruscan and Greek ear-rings could almost be models for the modern jewellery designer, too, and it has been known for visitors to Greek and Roman exhibits at many museums to get permission to copy every detail of an ancient design to be reproduced in modern ear-rings. More elaborate types of early Greek ear-rings consisted of horizontal half-cylinders made of gold wire, or plaited gold wire, with rosettes along the front upper edge, and pendant discs below. This form reappeared later as the disc ear-rings of swelling hoops with a pendant globular cluster and, later still, as the basket ear-ring of Etruria.

It was in the period following the Phoenician that the old processes were allied to a new geometric style. Ear-rings of that period featured stamping, granulation and even enamelling. Greece and Etruria produced ear-rings which terminated in heads of bulls and lions, with pendants in the form of lotus, pomegranate and palmettes. Some featured satyrs, sphinxes and sirens. Etruria brought the art of granulation to an amazing fineness and displayed an astonishing degree of skill and patience in this painstaking form of art. For it did need, above all things, a great deal of patience. First the pattern was drawn with infinite fidelity to detail in a field of minute grains and these were then fused into globules and soldered into position in a single operation.

This granulation was superseded by the Greeks in the fifth century B.C. by exquisite filigree work, quite often allied to beautifully delicate enamelling. In the third and second centuries B.C. Greek ear-rings carried tiny cast figures of animals and birds, while basket shapes, miniature vases and shells were also featured.

It is a curious fact that ear-rings were at first not allowed to be worn by the dignified citizens of Rome but were confined to the slaves who wore plain gold ear-rings and presumably so made clear their status. It was Julius Caesar who broke this custom and from then onwards Roman ear-rings assumed rich and intricate forms, using precious gems and inlays, becoming a vastly different 'status symbol' from those of the slaves.

At the beginning of the twelfth century the fashion of setting precious stones in ear-rings had not yet spread to Western Europe. In the Northern Hemisphere and in England women were apparently content with ear-rings consisting of a few coloured beads on a gold ring. When, in the Middle Ages, wimple headdresses and ear-covering coiffures were the fashion, ear-rings, if they were worn, were hidden from view.

The England of the Renaissance was an England awakening to the greatness of its native craftsmen, among whom, under royal patronage, the art of the jeweller-craftsmen burgeoned and flowered. After her royal father, Queen Elizabeth I gave the utmost impetus to the wearing of jewels of every kind. But she had a great predilection for pearl ear-rings (one famous pair of which have been mentioned in another chapter), and perhaps her favourite pair were round in shape, set with circular rubies *en cabochon* framed with pearls, from which hung long, pear-shaped pendants. Elizabeth I, with her long face, accentuated in its length by the height of her coiffures and head-dresses, defied all the rules by wearing ear-rings of extravagant length which by the law of Nature could only increase the effect of elongation. Since she was in essence a majestic and arrogant woman it may be that the effect was achieved deliberately.

During the seventeenth century the ear-ring continued to flourish in Britain, worn at this time by men as well as women. Charles I led the fashion for wearing a single ear-ring and followed it literally to the death, for he mounted the scaffold in Whitehall wearing a single pearl ear-ring on one ear. With his death, the fashion for men to wear ear-rings died too, except, oddly enough, among seafaring men and gipsies.

It was later in that century and during the eighteenth century that there was a considerable improvement in the art of gem-cutting. The setting of gems, too, improved and though they became less clearly defined than hitherto yet showed a rare delicacy. Diamonds, emeralds, sapphires and rubies were freely used. The fashions of the day collaborated in adding interest to the wearing of ear-rings, with low-cut décolletages and high-piled coiffures focusing attention on the ears. Small wonder then that the fashion for important, heavily jewelled ear-rings received great stimulation. 'Chandelier' ear-rings, as they are called today, were of extravagant length and width, sometimes being as long as three inches and as wide as two inches, practically touching the wearer's shoulders.

With the eighteenth century, too, came the parure—a matching suite of jewels—of which the ear-rings were an integral part. These suites of necklace, ear-rings, brooch, ring, bracelet, and sometimes a tiara also, featured great diversity of style and intricacy of design. Diamonds were the most popular gem for these, although sapphires, emeralds and rubies combined with diamonds were also very fashionable. But despite the advance at this time of the art of gem cutting not all ear-rings of this period were jewelled; many beautiful examples, unadorned by precious stones, achieved a colourful effect by exquisitely devised scrollwork in tinted gold, or with birds and flowers in coloured enamels.

The elongated drop ear-rings of the Directoire period were admirably suited to the dress fashions of the times. The Girandole, consisting of triple pendants, was often worn set with precious stones and has never entirely lost its popularity for formal occasions even to this day. Queen Victoria was many times painted wearing exquisite drop pendants in her ears and many modern formal ear-rings worn in the sixties of this century are direct descendants of the Victorian ear-rings of a hundred years ago.

The popularity of ear-rings continued throughout the nineteenth century and the fashion became more widespread with the lavish use of seed pearls and garnets (a much-loved Victorian fashion). Little girls had their ears pierced as a matter of course and it was quite usual to see enchantingly long skirted (and even longer-drawered) small girls wearing gold 'sleeper' ear-rings. The vogue is perpetuated in David Wilkie's picture 'The First Ears ring' showing a little girl of tender years having her ears pierced. A surprisingly large number of women performed this operation on their own ears themselves.

With the progress of the twentieth century the need for piercing the ears ceased to exist with the introduction of clip-on ear-rings. Women welcomed this not so much for the dispensation from ear-piercing which resulted but because it enabled them to use their ear-rings—or ear-clips—in other ways, as dress clips or lapel ornaments, and during the 'thirties and 'forties of this century it was a common practice to buy ear-clips in sets of four; one pair for wearing in the ears and the other for wearing as matching dress clips.

In contemporary times designs for ear-rings have taken the most eccentric and incredible forms so far as costume jewellery is concerned. The 'forties produced enormous gipsy-like circles which reached such dimensions that cartoonists depicted them

The late Mrs. Cornelius Vanderbilt wearing some of her multimillion-dollar collection of diamonds. Two of the Edwardian jewellery fashions shown here, the fringed corsage-garland and the diamond tiara, have almost disappeared.

Mrs. Geraldine Farrar, darling of the Metropolitan Opera during the early 1900s, wearing matched collar and tiara of diamonds in Egyptian lotus design. Note also the rings on both hands, even the index fingers being ornamented.

The formal corsage-garland, a jewellery form that has completely disappeared. It was worn swinging across the lower part of the evening bodice.

Diamond and sapphire necklace, property of H.R.H. the Princess Royal of Britain.

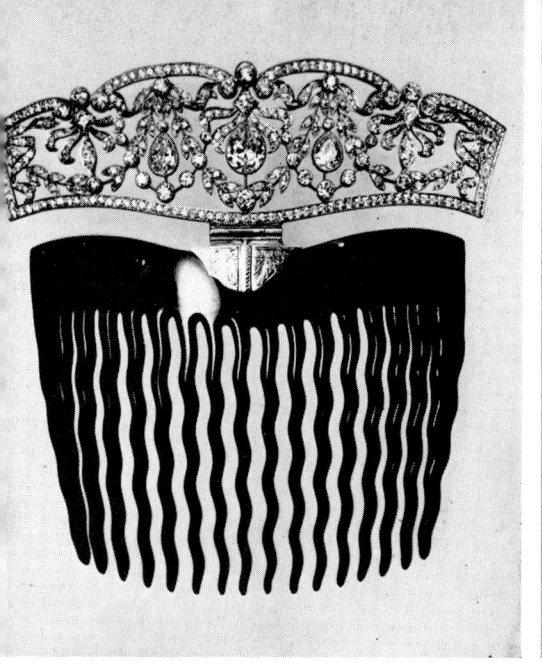

LEFT: A comb of tortoise shell with a hinged platinum ornament set with brilliant-cut diamonds. Made by Tiffany & Co. in 1910. RIGHT: Lady's watch and pin; white enamel dial with blue numerals, back encrusted with diamonds (c. 1880-1900). (Photographs by courtesy of the Metropolitan Museum of Art.)

LEFT: Hair ornament made of seventy-eight diamonds by Bick and Ostor of Montreal. RIGHT: A glittering river of diamonds make up this evening dress watch by Rolex of Switzerland.

Necklace of diamonds and sapphires created by Julius Cohen of New York. It can also be worn as two bracelets.

A nosegay of diamonds with five cultured pearls serves both as a necklace clasp and a cluster brooch. Primavesi and Kaufmann of Montreal were the creators.

with live birds swinging on them. Designs in the field of precious jewellery, however, followed a much more restrained pattern, though imaginative and stimulating. For formal wear the chandelier ear-ring returned to high favour and inventive designers produced elegant pendant ear-rings which were adaptable to both formal and informal wear, by the simple process of making the elaborate drop pendant part detachable, leaving a simple, single-stone clip for daytime wear. Many beautiful contemporary designs take the form of flowers in which rubies, emeralds, sapphires and diamonds provide the colour motif. There has been a return to the early Greek and Roman feeling in ear-clips composed of gold whorls and circles, with matching necklaces which surely owe their inspiration to the Celtic torques. The prevailing colour in fashion has always had its impact on contemporary jewellery, reflected today in the use of gold to harmonize with the browns and ambers which are a recurrent leitmotif in modern dress fashions.

But the diversity of patterns in modern ear-rings owes much to the many types discernible in the long history of ear ornamentation; in every design there is to be found an echo of the long-dead past—some borrowed from those craftsmen of nearly four thousand years ago.

CHAPTER SEVEN

Brooches and clips

BROOCHES began, like most decorative accessories, as a strictly functional adjunct to the toilette, probably as a thorn or a sharp piece of bone thrust through the material of the first rude garment to hold it together. A simple pin was not common in ancient times and its use for this purpose is a comparatively recent development. All brooches have evolved from the curved pin which in turn was most probably derived from a thorn. At an early period this form of pin, after having been passed through the garment, was, for greater security, bent up and its point caught behind its head. Later, in order that the point might be held more securely in the catch the pin was given a complete turn which produced the spring as it is now seen in our modern safety-pin. Constructed in this fashion the brooch, though in one piece, consisted of a 'fastened pin'.

From this primitive safety-pin, which is the foundation form of all brooches with a catch, developed the numerous varieties and patterns of the brooch or fibula which, instead of being constructed of one piece of metal, was of two pieces—the bow and the acus. This type of pin operated by means of a hinge, the result of gradually extending the coils of the spring symmetrically on each side of the pin into a double-twisted or bilateral spring and placing a bar through the coils. The T-shaped type of Roman provincial fibula common in France and Britain evolved from brooches hinged in this manner. The cruciform brooch of Anglo-Saxon times also originated from the early hinged brooch which was exclusively used until the revival of the safety-pin with a spring was patented as a new invention in the nineteenth century. In addition to these brooches and fibulae—all of which developed from the safety-pin type—there are three main groups of brooches: the circular disc type, the penannular or Celtic brooch, and the ring brooch.

The circular disc—the type in common use today—was originally in the form of a flat disc fitted with a hinged pin. Burial places dating from the early Iron Age which have been unearthed in Southern Europe have yielded examples of such circular plates fitted with a pin. These plates appear to have been developed by the conversion of a primitive disc of spiral concentric wire into a circular plate. The circular brooch of the Roman period, often inlaid with enamel, as well as the fine circular brooches of Anglo-Saxon times, have developed from these Iron Age ornaments.

In early ages, and even as late as Roman times, the bow or safety-pin type of brooch was more common than the disc and also more practical as it could easily hold the gathered folds of the garments worn in those days. In more recent times the disc-shaped brooch fitted with a hinged, or occasionally with a spring, pin has been more widely employed.

The two other principal groups of brooches—the Celtic brooch and the ring-brooch—are both developments of the simple pin in conjunction with a ring, in the case of the Celtic brooch, penannular, and in the case of the ring-brooch, annular. The Celtic brooch, with its pennannular ring and long pin, is apparently the result of fitting a pin to a prehistoric form of fastening for the dress—a penannular ring terminating with knobs known as a mammillary fibula. The ring brooch with complete ring and pin of the same length as the diameter of the ring, which achieved great popularity of use in medieval times, was the outcome of fitting a complete ring of wire to a pin to prevent the head of the pin slipping through the fabric. In time this ring became the more important part of the brooch.

In ancient Greece simple pins formed of gold wire were often employed as dress fastenings, while bow-shaped brooches were less frequently worn. Of the few gold brooches dating from the later Grecian periods which have been found most are characterized by a small arched bow and a long sheath for the pin-point, decorated with fine filigree designs. The gold fibulae of the Etruscans were usually in the form of a short arc-shaped bow and a long sheath for the pin, decorated with minute granular work, while the upper surfaces were often decorated with small animal models, a type of ornamentation much used at this time.

In addition to the more formal types of brooches the Roman colonists of Britain favoured many fancy devices of Celtic influence in the form of birds, fish and animals brilliantly coloured in enamels, the enamelling often being used to indicate the markings. Of all the Anglo-Saxon ornaments discovered, brooches were by far the most numerous. They had beauty and excellent workmanship and served as a basis for an important brooch form of the Middle Ages. The medieval brooch was generally a ring-brooch, the pin of which was held in position by the pull of the material through which it passed. There were many variations on the ring form and in some cases it was partially filled in, or its circle might be in the form of a wreath or a heart. Brooches worn by the wealthy during the Middle Ages were often quite magnificent jewels, enriched with gems set in delicate goldwork. An exquisite example of one of these early brooches can be seen in the Kunsthistorisches Museum, Vienna. Attributed to the Netherlands and dated *circa* 1450, this is in enamelled gold and represents a pair of lovers, the goldwork beautifully executed in spite of the early date.

Brooches were almost indispensable accessories to the Highland dress of medieval times; worn by both sexes, they fastened to the shoulder of the plaid. The earliest form of Scottish ring-brooch, during the thirteenth century, was a flattened circular ring, usually bearing talismanic Latin inscriptions generally of a religious nature. These inscriptions appeared on brooches dating from the thirteenth to the sixteenth centuries, but it would seem that the knowledge of Latin declined during the latter century, since the inscriptions on brooches of the later period were barely intelligible. In addition to circular brooches, many heart-shaped brooches have been found in Scotland. These were sometimes surmounted by a crown and occasionally set with jewels. Mainly intended as love-tokens and betrothal gifts, many of these brooches bore the word 'Love' on their reverse. These heart-shaped brooches are known as Luckenbooth brooches, presumably because they were commonly sold in the luckenbooths—the street stalls near St. Giles's Church in Edinburgh. They were usually pinned to the shawl worn by a child at its christening to ward off evil.

In the Renaissance period jewels were linked with the clothes fashions of the time, and with low-necked dresses and emphasis on the shoulders, the brooch, like the necklace and ear-ring, became an increasingly important jewel. Both men and women followed the fashion and wore brooches not only at the neck (where they had started as a fastening for the single garment) but at the waist, the shoulders and in the hat. Queen Elizabeth I inherited many wonderful brooches from Henry VIII and seldom, if ever, was painted without some magnificent example of this form of jewel. Henry VIII himself always wore a handsome jewelled brooch in the flat-topped hats he affected—the Tudor form of beret—with more brooches pinned to the shoulders of his tunic.

During the seventeenth and eighteenth centuries a notable change was seen in that jewels ceased to be a work of art with some fancy to be expressed and became much more of a medium of personal expression as an ornament, beautiful in thought and conception. They began to have a deeper significance and were often bespoken to express some personal attribute of the person for whom they were designed. It was an age of leisure and the craftsmen, unhurried in their work, were able to work painstakingly on jewels which had a personal theme to express and so called forth all their imagination to design. At this time, too, the art of gem cutting was more fully developed. Rose and brilliant cutting almost superseded table cutting and gave greatly added attractiveness to brooches of the period. For with the new interest in cutting the gems with which they were set jewels began to be much more fanciful in the form of their setting. There was a vogue for jewelled brooches in which the gems were set in solid lines to enhance their brilliance.

In the early Victorian age in Britain the most-liked brooches were those made of seed pearls mounted as bunches of grapes and other forms on mother of pearl; carved coral and ivory; and cameos. Whitby jet enjoyed a considerable vogue at the time of the Crimean War, a fashion greatly encouraged by Queen Victoria later on in her widowhood. Girandole brooches, consisting of a large central gem from which smaller versions of the same gems were suspended by short closely linked chains, were both handsome and effective—and command good prices when they can be found today. Bow and knot brooches set with turquoise and pearls appeared in many charming and fanciful designs and there was a fashion for large carbuncles and *cabochon* almadine garnets with a superimposed star of silver or seed pearls. Sometimes these superimposed stars were set on a background of rich blue enamel in round and oval shapes. Pendeloque pearls, tassels of gold and silver, and sometimes pear-shaped *cabochon* gems were worn suspended from some brooches of this period.

The Mid-Victorian brooches favoured round and oval shapes rather than the rectangular, usually with a wide gold or silver border richly decorated around a large central stone. Brooches representative of sporting interests made their appearance, mostly in the form of miniature hunting crops, horseshoes, crossed whips and foxes' masks. ,

Late Victorian (1885–1901) brooches showed a growing liking for more colour, more precious gems, more romantic designs. Birds, butterflies, flowers, dragonflies and many other fauna and flora were represented in diamonds and other gems. These ranged in size from quite small pieces to large corsage brooches. Many used coloured enamels to follow Nature's colouring and as a contrast there was also a fashion for simple little gold brooches in the form of a wishbone—or merrythought—usually set with a single pearl. Crescents and stars set with diamonds in gold were a brooch fashion, some of which were worn in the hair. Bow brooches from which hung brightly coloured enamel or gem-set fob watches were a delightful fashion of this age.

Across the Channel the new régime created many new fashions

in jewellery. Crescents, stars and 'half-moons' of diamonds formed the popular brooches of the day, again worn in the hair as well as on the corsage. The Empress Josephine had set the fashion for cameo brooches and there was for a time a galaxy of these 'jewels', never since equalled.

With the opening of the twentieth century the 'Century' brooch was launched, composed of a diamond-set star with radiating spikes of gold bearing the figures '1901' in diamonds. 'Cauduceus' brooches of classical inspiration were designed in gold set with rubies and emeralds on the central rod, with diamond-set mercury wings and with a large pearl at the top and bottom of the rod. Brooches with a nautical flavour were fashionable and were made in the shapes of small anchors and yachts, diamond-set. The range of sporting interests having widened, sporting brooches in the form of bicycles, golf clubs, tennis rackets and so on were worn in the ties which the sportswomen of the Edwardian era wore with their masculine-type shirt blouses.

As the century progressed brooches were made in a 'modern' design, usually rectangular, gem-set, in representational form of which one may be quoted as a typical example. This consisted of a frame of diamonds in which was represented a diamond umbrella, fully opened, with slanting drops of 'rain' of diamonds. These brooches in all their variations were two-dimensional. A daring innovation was the introduction of the brooch in the form of a pair of clips, to be worn as one single brooch, or divided up to wear as two matching clips. These were becoming a well-established fashion by the 'thirties and just as the designers were really getting down to the creation of more imaginative styles in three dimensions, the Second World War intervened and their talents were turned elsewhere—to fine precision work on weapons of war.

In the years since that war ended there have been immense strides forward in the design of jewellery in which brooches have had their full share of the artists' creative talent. Once gold became more freely available (its use had been almost entirely withdrawn during the war) there was a great vogue for gold representations of flowers and more formal designs. At this period the use of gold wire became widespread in the fashioning of lapel brooches of bizarre design, lightly set with precious gems and with the interest focused more on the metal than the stones. Of recent years, however, precious gems, and in particular diamonds, have been more and more used; the technique of the 'sixties has gone into reverse and is concentrated on showing gems and keeping the settings almost invisible. One exception is the 'cloth of gold' jewellery made from gold wire pulled to the thickness of a thread and woven like thread into a supple gold fabric which is used for bow brooches with a central motif of diamonds and other precious gems.

CHAPTER EIGHT

Tiaras and hair ornaments

IT is a fascinating reflection that the flashing diamond tiara which is today an indication of the grandeur of the social occasion, most probably had its origin in the band which primitive people wore around their heads to keep their uncut hair out of their eyes. Since that time head-dresses have grown immensely more important and significant and of all forms of jewellery they have splendidly survived both as a decoration and as an insignia of rank.

In the Bronze Age women wore pins in their hair, while centuries before the Celts came, even older races were making head coverings of hammered gold, using the pure metal. Diadems and varied head ornaments were worn in ancient Mycenae, some decorated with enormous drop ornaments which may have been the forerunner of ear-rings. Early Greek women wore ornamental hairpins in embossed and repoussé work. Ladies of high rank, however, were much more grand and their head ornaments took the form of elaborate golden crowns, while their hairpins were richly made in the form of animals, goddesses and flowers.

As any serious student of the history of dress will know, diadems and fillets played an important part in the toilette of the Roman matron. When her hair had been elaborately dressed and coiffed by her slaves she would further adorn its coils and swathes with pearls, precious stones and other ornaments, as well as long, intricately designed hairpins. A magnificent gold diadem from a set said to have been found in a tomb at Madytos on the Hellespont, *circa* 350 B.C., can be seen in the Metropolitan Museum of Art, New York. This and other examples of early Roman head jewellery show great imagination in the use of gold repoussé work.

With changes in fashions came changes in the forms of hair jewels. From the tenth to the sixteenth century women adorned their heads with fillets, chaplets and simple bands, while the young girls wore youthful wreaths of natural flowers or more permanent chaplets made of gold set with precious gems. As time went on these head-dresses became more massive, and some were sentimentally modelled on the hinged belts worn by the knights of the period. Within this time—in the fourteenth century—a fashion arose for exquisite circlets set with precious stones, further adorned with *fleur-de-lis*, crosses and similar motifs. It was from these that the coronets which today denote different ranks in the peerage were probably developed.

Famous Italian painters of the fourteenth and fifteenth centuries portray ladies wearing the *ferronnière*—a head ornament consisting of a narrow cord or band worn around the head with a single beautiful jewel suspended from it so as to lie in the centre of the forehead. This simplicity later gave way, in the sixteenth century, to more magnificent forms of head-dresses sparkling with jewels, and to ropes of pearls twisted cunningly into the coiffures which were another fashion much followed.

In England the Tudor Queen Elizabeth I brought the art of hair ornamentation literally to a high peak. Europe in general at that time sponsored elaborate head-dresses, but Elizabeth I outshone them all, not only by reason of her intricately and heavily jewelled head-dresses in which pearls predominated, but with magnificent hairpins known at that time as 'bodkyns'. One of her prized jewels was a 'bodkyn golde garnished at the ende and 4 smale diamondes and a smale rubye with a crown of ophales and a very smale perle pendant peare fashione' as it is faithfully described in the inventory of the Queen's jewels. These 'bodkyns', or hairpins, were fascinating in their variety, and in the intricacy and imagination of their design. One way of wearing the hairpin was to thrust it through the rim of a hat so that the jewelled head of the pin rested on the forehead to make an attractive ornament near the face.

During the eighteenth century, sponsored by France, the headdress reached an advanced stage in its development. Frenchwomen in particular favoured the elegant jewelled aigrette with precious stones in a setting of great lightness. These jewelled aigrettes were in the form of birds, butterflies, bows and flowers mounted on fine spirals of precious metal so that the jewels sparkled and quivered with the slightest movement. Marie Antoinette is reputed to have been foremost in the fashion for wearing jewelled hairpins and aigrettes composed entirely of diamonds in the very lightweight settings.

With the coming of the nineteenth century frontlets and diadems, jewelled hair combs and hairpins, all richly gem-set, triple chains and strings of pearls were worn in the hair. The *ferronnière* staged a return to fashion though sometimes a fine gold chain took the place of the silk cord or band of ribbon of Quattrocento Italy. This was tied at the back of the head or, in the case of a gold chain, pinned, with a single jewel hanging on the forehead.

At this time cameos came very much into the picture and women wore tiaras and diadems set with cameos, with matching necklace and ear-rings similarly set. High combs were also set with cameos. These combs were of exaggerated height so that when they were worn thrust into the hair at the back they stood up over the top of the coiffure in full view from every angle. The high comb of the Empire period, set with upright rows of pearls and coral, was a favoured form of hair decoration at this time as can be seen from examples in the French museums.

From the time of the earliest head ornaments, their design and form have been determined by the coiffure of the day. Thus, in the twentieth century, during the reign of King Edward VII, imposing tiaras, chiefly diamond-set and of a rather massive character were worn perched on the rather heavy frontal coiffure of that time. The fringed hair-style favoured by the lovely Queen Alexandra led to the fashion for diamond 'fenders' which are among treasured heirloom jewels in some of Britain's oldest families. Not all women, however, followed the fringe fashion. More often the hair was worn in a rolled pompadour and into this were pinned jewelled hair slides or barettes in the form of crescents, stars, butterflies and small birds. Sometimes as many as half a dozen of these would be placed strategically in the 'bird's nest' coiffure of elaborate curls and quiffs. They must have looked quite enchanting.

A decade or so later—coming into the 'twenties—tiaras were worn low on the forehead, composed chiefly of diamonds in rich flower designs, sometimes having a flower-shaped corsage brooch to match. For the first time tiaras began to be made to follow the shape of the head, curving to fit more closely and more comfortably. As the hair shortened into the shingle and Eton crop, puffs and curls disappeared and with them the tiara, except on formal and Court occasions. Logically enough, as hair was cropped, so were head-dresses. Jewelled combs disappeared from fashion to be entirely superseded by diamond slides, barettes and bandeaux, the latter worn flat on the forehead, the former holding the forward-curving piece of hair known at that time as the 'kiss curl'.

During the 'thirties, with hair being worn longer and fuller, there was a resurgence of the tiara fashion, although not on the scale of Edwardian days. Then came the war and the years of austerity. Hair once again was close-cropped; the social scene dimmed, and tiaras and jewelled hair ornaments were relegated to bank vaults and family safes.

The economic 'hang-over' of the war lasted an astonishingly long time and it was not until the 'fifties that the social barometer began to show signs of being set fair. Sparked off by state visits from foreign royalty and state leaders, social events began again to take on some of the glitter and pomp which had characterized, pre-eminently, the Edwardian era of social gaiety. Of this resurgence the tiara and jewelled hair ornament was the highlight in every way. Not only did the family heirlooms come once more into the social scene; jewellers began to create modern ones and to find a ready market for them—but with an outstanding characteristic—their tiaras were all made to be convertible into several different pieces of jewellery. An outstanding example of this trend was the Coronation Suite, made by a leading jewellery designer-craftsman to commemorate the coronation of Queen Elizabeth II in 1953. The tiara, necklace and bracelet of this magnificent diamond and platinum suite were all convertible to be worn as nine different pieces of jewellery. The permutations of the suite were seemingly endless and were designed to provide different jewels for every possible social occasion and time of day.

Today the fashionable woman's 'crowning glory' proudly bears a modern 'crown' of jewels and the contemporary social scene is correspondingly enriched, to the delight of the wearer, the beholder, and the jeweller-craftsman.

CHAPTER NINE

Regency and Victorian jewellery

FASHIONS in jewellery have been traced, superficially perhaps, from thousands of years ago, and what emerges is the curious fact that in all those centuries none has shown such a definite 'period' as the century and a half covered by the late Regency and Victorian eras. This may be due to the survival of so much of the actual jewellery worn by all classes of society, and to the fact that from the mid-nineteenth century the new 'art' of photography and the development of illustrated fashion journals provided authentic evidence of jewel as well as of dress fashions. The stability of the country and its settled prosperity also contributed towards providing a fairly complete and detailed record of the times. Britain, domestically, was pre-eminently a self-contained community. The social scene was set within a circumscribed area; entertaining was largely a home affair, its focal point the Royal Court, its branches spreading to the home, the theatre, the ball and the garden party. Concentrated as it was within these limits of expression Victorian fashion in all its forms was noted, written about and illustrated with a detailed minuteness which is immensely rewarding to the researcher.

Nevertheless there remain some misconceptions about the period. One is that it was a 'stodgy' time, stuffy, heavy and stolid. Judged by comparison with the mercurial 'here today, tomorrow in Europe, Fiji or Australia' travel-minded twentieth century, with the 'live today, for tomorrow we may have the atom bomb' uncertainty and insecurity of modern times, the adjectives applied to the Victorian age have a blissfully secure and stable ring.

Whatever may be the contemporary judgement on Victorian times, Victorian jewellery is not to be dismissed as heavy and clumsy as many people mistakenly imagine it to have been. Indeed, some of it was extremely delicate and elegant. And, too, the use of what are called 'semi-precious' stones (which are more correctly described as 'gemstones' in the trade)—those other than the five main precious gems, rubies, diamonds, sapphires, emeralds and pearls—made quite enchanting jewellery. Their consequently relatively low cost made them of little intrinsic value, a fact that explains why so many of them have survived. Where, in a time of financial stress, precious gem-set jewellery might be sold, the gemstone-set jewellery was considered to be of too little value to fetch anything worth the selling. And again, it was often not thought worth while, when Regency and Victorian jewellery had been inherited, to have it remodelled in more modern styles.

As a result, there is happily a wide field of selection for the searcher after jewels of these periods, though with the passage of time they have acquired value as antiques and are commensurately more and more costly to buy. Apart from their antique value, however, some jewels of these two periods are really exquisite; others have an irresistible charm as relics of what was perhaps the only really peacefully prosperous age Britain has known.

It was an age of the bourgeoisie in which the middle-class tradespeople flourished. Family businesses were being built up and the comfortably-circumstanced burghers lavished suites and parures of jewels on their equally comfortable wives. It was an age of class-consciousness and differentiation, but it did have one really admirable characteristic which has to some extent vanished with *autre temps autre mœurs*—Victorians liked whatever they had to be the real thing. Thus, though they did not aspire to the diamonds and precious gems of the 'gentry' as the aristocracy was described, they insisted on the real thing in what was termed 'semi-precious' stones. From the psychological aspect this attitude holds the clue to the sturdy, feet-on-the-ground character of the Victorians, one which cannot but be admired. Psychological and sociological aspects aside, the Victorians had a wealth of choice in the field of contemporary jewellery and the popularity of the lesser-known topaz, amethyst, tourmaline, peridot, amber, garnet—the list is endless—gave the

Georgian and Victorian jewellers immense scope for their carefully hand-made creations. The 'poor relation' of the marble-sized Orient pearl—seed pearl—was freely used for the most delightful jewellery, worked into intricate designs to form sets of ear-rings, necklaces, bracelets (usually in pairs) and brooches. Jet was another 'gem' much used in the late Victorian period, an inevitable concomitant of the extremely long period of mourning which was observed at the time by a bereaved family. In this Queen Victoria played an important part. Her period of mourning for her Consort, Prince Albert, was in fact so prolonged that it led to great restiveness among the tradespeople and perhaps among the jeweller-craftsmen, too, for it imposed a surprisingly (to the modern mind) sobering and restraining effect on the contemporary social scene. This was the period of the mourning ring, brooches encasing a lock of the departed's hair, or with the hair woven intricately to form a pattern for the brooch. It was, too, the jet age—but how far removed from the modern connotation of that term. From the full mourning, or jet, period (usually a full year) to the half-mourning (six to nine months), or amethyst, period only those colours were worn, so seriously did the Victorians follow the conventions. In this, as in every period of history, the domestic and social structure is definable by the type of jewellery then in vogue. It makes a fascinating study.

While Georgian jewellery was either extremely solid, using both gold and silver freely, or of a more lighthearted character where diamond jewels were concerned, the Victorian era opened up in an ambience of prosperity in which Romanticism flourished. Languid Lydias pierced their elaborate coiffures with jewelled pins, butterflies, crescent moons, daggers—all with telling effect. The *ferronnière* expressed the height of the Romantic mood and was adopted with great *empressment* by the early Victorian misses. With a romantic mood what more natural than that the designers should seek inspiration from the colourful social scene across the Channel? French jewellers found a ready market in Britain for their jewels in which, at this time, medieval motifs played an important part. Enamel, niello, and carved gem work were produced in profusion in the fourth, fifth and sixth decades of Queen Victoria's reign. Coral came into fashion with a flourish; not the branched, natural-shaped coral (though this was used, and very effectively), but beautifully carved and shaped pieces which were used to make parures of tiara, necklace, brooch, and bracelets *en suite*. Berries and flowers were made of coral, extravagant sprays of flowers and leaves were carved to represent nature and made enchanting jewellery, much sought after today by collectors of Victoriana. Though the coral itself came from Naples mainly, British jewellers themselves fashioned the gemstone into jewellery. One of them, Robert Phillips, was so successful with his coral jewellery that he was decorated by the then King of Italy for his work.

Coincidental with the coral vogue of early Victorian days was the vogue for seed pearls. Brooches, bracelets, necklaces, rings, and ear-rings were made of massed seed pearls, while cameos and miniatures were frequently set in a surround of these tiny pearls. Necklaces of coral beads or tiny twigged coral branches (such as Queen Elizabeth II and Princess Anne wore) and of seed pearls were the recognized presents for a new baby girl. Cameos came into high fashion and so did mosaic jewels. In cameos the paramount design was that of the twin figures of Night and Day, but other mythological subjects were freely featured in these carved shells. This fashion found a sponsor in the young Queen Victoria and so ensured a following from her devoted subjects. To this queen's love of Scotland the period owed the fashion for cairngorm-set jewellery, the favourite expression of which was the silver brooch in the form of a thistle, the 'brush' of which was represented by a cairngorm, an amethyst, or a topaz. Scottish pebble brooches were much worn and a dreary fashion they were—one which even a craze for Victoriana cannot make appealing.

The period has been referred to as 'peaceful' but no century in history has entirely passed without a war of some kind. Now it was the Crimean War, and though it did not impinge to any degree on the broad social scene, there were unhappily casualties among the British soldiers fighting there and in consequence many families were in the deep mourning the times demanded. Hence the somewhat horrid fashion for memento jewellery enclosing human hair. Some of these were of extreme morbidity in conception; brooches in the form of tombs and funereal wreaths were lugubriously worn and in order to ensure that only the dear departed's locks were used, early Victorian young ladies devoted themselves to the gruesome task of placing the hair in its locket, pendant, or brooch container, not trusting the jeweller to abstain from using any hair available.

Towards the middle of the nineteenth century a metal called pinchbeck was much used for jewellery. It had the look of gold, though it contained none, and it continued to be used a great deal until the development of the South African gold mines brought the precious metal into freer use. Cut steel was also used at this particular time.

In the field of precious jewellery of the early Victorian era much use was made of large diamonds, seen in handsome parures and smaller suites. Gem cutting and setting had not achieved their present skills. Cascades and waterfalls were the favoured motifs, while the Georgian and early Victorian 'fenders'—as the tiaras of this period were called—used flowers, leaves and wheat ears as the dominant diamond motifs. Baguette cutting had not been adopted and those diamonds used were usually rose or brilliant cut.

This was the period when the mobile setting was adopted for 'trembling' hair ornaments and brooches. The method of achieving movement was similar to that of the mid-twentieth century—a fine spiral spring attaching the jewel to its pin or clasp. Turquoises were in fashion, seen set in cluster rings, in ear-rings, in the large gold entwined serpents which formed contemporary bracelets, in ribband brooches and in necklaces. Usually set in gold, they were invariably companioned by pearls, though sometimes they were allied to coral for more colourful jewels. Flexible gold chains were in fashion, especially for necklaces which had festooned chains from which hung five or six jewelled pendants at regular intervals.

Mid-nineteenth-century Victoriana also included large corsage ornaments which might be entirely diamond-set in the form of a life-size flower spray complete with leaves, or a ribbon bow with diamond cascade and a central coloured precious gem, or a baroque style using large carbuncles with diamond cascades. A favourite design of this period, easily dated, is the corsage ornament with a very large upper part holding perhaps a topaz, amethyst, carbuncle or similar stone from which hung triple gold chains, holding a smaller facsimile of the upper part of the ornament. Bracelets were wide, ornate and intricately twisted. For these the serpent was the dominant motif, the undulations, twists and tapering form of these reptiles lending themselves to the designs of the day. The heavily coiled snake would be of gold set perhaps with just two emeralds for 'eyes' or set all over with turquoise or garnets, or seed pearls. Queen Victoria had one of the former type which is believed to be the one which Princess Margaret has sometimes worn. The flexible nature of the bracelet made it possible for it to be worn coiled closely around the wrist, or opened out to twine round the arm from wrist to just below the elbow. Other bracelet styles were composed of five or six rows of flexible gold chains, with a painted miniature as the clasp, or the same number of rows of pearls or other gemstones.

With the third quarter of the nineteenth century, the mid-Victorian period, jewellery became more colourful. Several jewellery designers became notable and provided literal gems of creative artistry. In the van was Giuliano, who settled in London from his native Naples and who, together with his colleague Robert Phillips, gave expression to the jewellery art of the time. In their designs they achieved a colourful effect by the juxtaposition of unusual gem combinations. For example, in a pendant necklace which Giuliano made, the necklace itself is of pearls set in red enamel and gold, with a central pendant of golden topaz, pearls and cairngorms and an intricate background of dark red, white, vermilion, green and black enamel. Corals, diamonds and emeralds were another unusual colour combination.

This was the period when the comb was literally high fashion. Blonde tortoiseshell formed the teeth and frame, while the top of the comb, designed to appear over the high-dressed coiffure, was embellished in many ways. There was the row of large pearls; the row of tortoiseshell spheres; the enamelled classical representations after the Greek; the carved coral 'acorns'; the jewelled diadem; and the crystal-set top, as well as the diamond-set motifs.

Bracelets still continued the serpent theme, but broad, flat circlets began to be seen, sometimes of equal width all round, sometimes with graduated width, wide in front and narrow at the back, the wider part being either profusely ornamented or gem-set. Some had lozenge-shaped panels, in the centre of each of which was set a precious stone or gemstone. Silver bangles were generally made with an ornately cut and chased border enclosing a simply etched design, usually of some simple woodland flower. Diamond bracelets followed the style of having width in the centre front, tapering towards the clasp. These were set in gold, which in itself helps to date them (1860–70). The jeweller-craftsman demonstrated his skill then, as he does today, by making the central motif detachable for wearing as a brooch.

In gems the mid-Victorian period began to exploit the supply of the five primary precious stones, and emeralds, rubies, sapphires and pearls joined with diamonds in forming fine jewels. Differently coloured golds began to be used, adding their colour to the enamels and coloured gems that were making this one of the most interesting and versatile periods of jewellery. The designer often took his designs from life and created representations of birds, bees, flowers, butterflies, dragonflies (these had a tremendous success), swans, and other fauna and flora. Ear-rings varied between the stud type set with seed pearls, garnets, turquoise, and, of course, diamonds, to the 'chandelier' hanging two or three inches in length from the ear-lobe. Pagodas, tassels, and bells in gold were in great vogue as ear-rings in the 'sixties, while gold-fringed medallions in which tiny diamonds or pearls were set were another mid-Victorian fashion. Fancy belt buckles, châtelaines, fan chains, sleeve links were also part of the jewellery of the 'sixties. Quite small girls began to wear ear-rings for which their ears, like their mothers', were pierced.

Coming to the late Victorian era the styles show that the influence of Giuliano was still apparent in the use of colour. Moonstones came into fashion at this time and the Italian craftsman used these milky-white stones to great effect combined with amethysts and blue-coloured enamels to make a fringed necklace, *circa* 1890. Châtelaines were in high fashion, usually in silver or pinchbeck, the utilitarian constituents such as scissors, keys, button-hook, vinaigrette, being augmented by the purely decorative, such as models of flowers and other representations. The aim at this time appeared to be to have as many attachments as possible to the châtelaine (itself an ornate creation). Belt buckles became very decorative and were rivalled in their ornamentation of chased and applied work by the double clasps used for fastening a cloak or coat at the throat. Links of gold set with jewels and attached by a fine gold chain were used to secure the fichu or lace collar worn high at the throat. Hearts appeared everywhere, as rings, brooches, pendants, and lockets, either in outline or solid shape. Some of the latter were completely pavé set with seed pearls, diamonds, or turquoises. Gem-set bracelets superseded the wide gold and silver bands of the mid-Victorian period and where the serpent design persisted, it was now seen set with diamonds throughout its entire length.

Inevitably with the enormous hats of the close of the nineteenth century, hatpins came into fashion and the contemporary jeweller 'went to town' with these new accessories. Necessarily of a frightening length (hat crowns were sometimes as wide as twelve inches across) the heads of hatpins rioted with intricate and fanciful designs. Garnet-set crescents, plumed helmets in silver and gold, outspread fans decorated with intricate figures, cherubs, medallions, shells, mythological figures—there was an infinite variety of choice. Many were richly set with precious stones and gemstones, and were often enamelled, too.

The beautiful Princess Alexandra had arrived on the social scene some years before as the bride of the Prince of Wales and had introduced a livelier note to a society whose gaiety was later somewhat restricted by Queen Victoria's sustained mourning and semi-retirement. The wind of change brought a new magnificence. There was a more massive type of jewellery to be seen of which the stomacher of diamonds (of eighteenth-century origin), sometimes eight or ten inches in length and about three or four inches wide at its centre; the sautoir (a diamond necklace, long and narrow, from which depended a handsomely large cross set with large diamonds, pendant, or tassel, also diamond-set), were striking examples. There were the diamond 'dog-collars', wide bands worn close to the base of the throat, which were the Princess's own fashion. Tiaras, higher and more imposing; immense shoulder knots set with diamonds; huge floral diamond sprays—all contributed a lavish social background to the Boer War—a curious contrast to the austere social background of the two wars of the next century.

At this time women were becoming emancipated from the drawing-room and salon. They began playing golf; they were taking an active part in grouse and pheasant shoots and the late-Victorian jeweller was not slow to profit from the new trends. Sporting brooches of miniature golf clubs, or topped with miniature heads of game birds, made their appearance. Some were in gold, others were richly set with precious gems. Hatpins with ends in the shape of miniature golf clubs or hockey sticks appeared. Finding their new freedom of physical movement impeded by the flowing skirts of the time, these sportswomen found a way of lifting the hems decorously by using a miniature facsimile hand, with hinged clip like an office file. This was used to grip firmly the folds of the skirt so that the hem just cleared the ground. Here again the enterprising jeweller found an outlet for his talents and created skirt clips of great versatility in design as well as usefulness.

Meanwhile, with the royal occasions setting the scene for brilliant displays of jewellery in Britain, what of the rich New World on this side of the Atlantic? With no Royal Family to inspire scenes of great grandeur and ceremonial, yet with enormous sources of wealth opening up on every hand, it was left to the wealthy socialites of the United States to lead jewel fashions. And they did so with magnificent results. Not for them, at that time, the home-produced jewels; their spectacular gems came from the fashion centres of Europe and presented a truly dazzling spectacle.

In the mid-nineteenth century American jewellery was machine-made (or factory, as it was called) though there was growing up in 1850 a jewel industry located around Providence, Rhode Island. Nevertheless a limited amount of fine jewellery was being produced in workshops belonging to a few of the great retailers. Tiffany were making a limited amount of their own jewels, as were Galt's of Washington (established in 1802 at Alexandria, Virginia); Stowell in Boston in 1822; Jaccard's in St Louis in 1829; and Caldwell's in Philadelphia in 1839. Some of the records of the fine jewellery these firms made still exist, showing a fascinating range of designs of historical interest to the student of jewel fashions. Most of the jewellery of this period, however, came to America from Paris. Of the jewels of that period that were typically American were the 'nuggets of gold' of 1849–1880, made from lumps of quartz and sometimes of pebbles of pure gold found in California by the Forty-niners. 'Everything gold became the fashion back East,' records one writer. 'Every woman wanted a brooch or bracelet of "Californy" gold nuggets. Like the discovery of the great new fields of diamonds in South Africa in the 1870's, the finding of gold in our own backyard inspired new designing of jewellery. San Francisco jewellers sold gold-quartz jewels all through the '70s and '80s, the greenish quartz heavily flecked with yellow gold was set in solid gold for contrast . . .'

With the advent of the 1900's the gushing oil wells of Texas set the Texan owners buying diamond-studded belts of embossed cowhide, the flowers of the design being formed of diamonds and having larger diamonds set in the heavily carved buckles of white gold. The store of a Dallas jeweller, founded in 1897, specialized in these diamond belts and also made miniature oil derricks of white diamonds with 'gushers' of yellow diamonds. Charms in the form of maps of Texas had the leading oilfields marked out in diamonds.

Throughout the nineteenth century beautiful silver, turquoise, garnet and enamel jewellery made by the Indians in the Southwest contributed their own designs, symbols, colouring and materials to the jewellery of the period.

From 1883 onwards a new focal point was found as the 'proving ground' of everything new and ultra in jewels, gowns, furs, tiaras and head-dresses. As there was no Royal Court and the White House had never been a centre of fashion, the 'Diamond Horseshoe' of the Metropolitan Opera House became the venue for showing off the newest and loveliest of jewels and fashions. It became the place where 'Society' sat and glittered, to see and be seen. An appearance at the Opera House in 'full fig' was equivalent to attendance at a Royal Court in Europe. The élite had no titles but they could buy tiaras that looked like crowns; they could bow to each other even if they could not curtsey to a reigning Royalty—and they had the money to have a right royal time and present a right royal appearance. Wealth was literally gushing out of the ground in the form of gold, copper and oil. 'Mrs Nouveau-Riche jostled Mrs Old-Name for a place in the social gaslight of the period'—and there was only, until 1883, the substantial and well-patronized opera house in Union Square; the old Academy of Music, with but nine socially desirable boxes.

This clearly was inadequate for a society bursting at its seams with ever-increasing wealth and power. William Vanderbilt, backed by the ninety million dollars he had inherited from his father, Commodore Vanderbilt; Darius Ogden Mills, newly arrived from gold-filled California; William Rockefeller, brother of John D., the oil king; Jay Gould, the financial wizard, and other millionaires decided to build their own opera house—up on Broadway where the horse-cars had their terminus. The sum they pledged was six hundred thousand dollars but the finished job cost two million dollars for an opera house that covered a whole block—but there were many boxes, banked in tiers three deep with more tucked in on the sides. A hundred and twenty all told, in the form of a horseshoe facing the stage on the plan of the famous opera houses of Europe. Sixty-five stockholders drew lots to decide who would sit where, and, on the opening night of October 22, 1883, with the Goelets, the Astors, the Vanderbilts, the Drexels and the Morgans sitting in their respective boxes the newspapers estimated the average wealth per box as around nine million dollars. So much money, plus the gold-painted décor, earned the glittering semicircle the title of the Golden Horseshoe. After the disastrous fire of 1892 thirty-five millionaires put up sixty thousand dollars each towards the rebuilding and in return became life owners of the thirty-five most coveted boxes in the lower tier. On the gala reopening in November 1893, ten thousand new electric bulbs turned the Horseshoe into a diamond-studded necklace, and with an estimated one hundred and seventy million dollars worth of diamonds worn by the occupants, the Golden Horseshoe was appropriately renamed the 'Diamond Horseshoe'.

Among the leading Society women in the pre-World War I period was the late Mrs Cornelius Vanderbilt who owned a million-dollar collection of diamonds which included a type of jewel not seen in Britain—a fringed corsage-garland of diamonds, an incredible jewel which has completely disappeared from fashion. This was worn swinging right across the lower part of the evening gown bodice, with deep fringe, tassels and bow knots, all in diamonds. Another version of this wholly American jewel was worn by the late Mrs William H. Shieffelin (May Jay) in the 1870's. Hers took the form of seven looped rows of quite large pearls across the bodice of an off-the-shoulders evening gown. It is interesting to note that both these ladies wore with these immensely important corsage jewels utterly unrelated choker necklaces and tiaras—unrelated in design and in the case of Mrs Shieffelin of unrelated gems too. In an old woodcut showing a scene at a fashionable daytime wedding in a Fifth Avenue church, New York, in the 1870's, in which full evening toilette is worn without hats, none of the elegantly apparelled ladies wears a corsage ornament. Almost all wear a fashion prevalent in mid-Victorian England—jewelled flowers and ornaments in the hair and (again an English vogue) carried a fan, usually jewelled. The engagement ring of this period was usually a diamond cluster made up of a lot of small stones rather than a single large one, with a broad gold wedding ring heavily chased after the style of the British keeper ring.

Nineteenth-century American jewellery included items which had their counterpart in Britain. Old jewellery catalogues show ladies' vest chains, onyx and jet parures, hair jewellery (but imitation, not the human hair used in Britain), fancy key winders for old watches (often gem-set), lyre-shaped ear-rings. Peculiar to American jewellery, however, were the bracelets with 'sea-beans' and imitation elks' teeth.

From the 1890's to the 1930's the most fashionable betrothal symbol in the United States was the solitaire diamond ring. First in a rather solid gipsy mounting, the diamond progressed to a somewhat lighter belcher-type setting with prongs, then to an eight-prong and finally to a six-prong 'Tiffany' mounting. Around 1895 the plain high yellow gold mounting with six prongs to hold the stone was shown by Tiffany and became so firmly established as the correct engagement ring that Tiffany style mountings were made by many manufacturers. The prongs reached their highest elevation about 1928 when a sizeable diamond might be lifted almost half an inch above the finger level—all in yellow gold. The date is important, for in 1929 the United States suffered the Great Depression and from that time through the 1930's the size of the solitaire diamond diminished because no one could afford the single large stone. To meet the need for a large-seeming stone the central diamond was built up with small diamonds (mêlée) at each side.

Somewhat earlier—in about 1905—a new bridal ring fashion was introduced in America by a Detroit firm named Traub who began to make wedding rings of gold carved with a design of orange blossoms. A few years later they brought out a diamond-set engagement ring which was also carved with an orange blossom design. This was the beginning of 'matched sets' of engagement and wedding rings.

The fob watch of Victorian times, so popular in Britain, had its counterpart in American jewellery. Like the British version these fob watches and their brooches were usually in coloured enamel and were diamond-set. An example made by Tiffany, *circa* 1880–1900, had the brooch in the form of a serpent, diamond-set, the watch itself having a white enamelled dial with blue numerals and steel hands, the back of the watch being encrusted with diamonds, brilliant cut. Another fashion equally popular on both sides of the Atlantic in the Edwardian or pre-World War I period was the high jewelled comb. Tiffany exhibited a charming example in a 'Turn of the Century' exhibition held in New York in 1948 which they had made in 1910. This was in tortoiseshell with a hinged platinum ornament across the top pierced in a design of pear-shaped drops, leaf and ribbon motifs —all diamond-set.

CHAPTER TEN

Some royal jewels

It is a curious anomaly that H.M. Queen Elizabeth II, as a private person, has simple, unostentatious tastes, yet she is the possessor of perhaps the most wonderful collection of jewels of any woman in the world. And this excludes the Crown Jewels and Regalia which are almost exclusively the property of the state.

Until her marriage and her subsequent accession to the throne Queen Elizabeth II owned surprisingly few jewels and wore even fewer. Many of her contemporaries in the upper stratum of society had far more jewellery than had Princess Elizabeth, which was clearly as she wished. Her favourite jewels were of sentimental interest with family associations, such as the simple string of pearls which she wore—a gift from her father, King George VI—at her parents' coronation and later, in her teens, the three-row necklace of modestly sized pearls given her by her grandfather, King George V, and the tiny watch set in a bracelet of thirty-two tiny squares of platinum which her father and mother brought back with them as a gift of the people of France after their state visit to Paris in 1938. This latter jewel the Queen wore constantly and it was a matter of great regret to her when she lost it one day in 1955 when walking her dogs at Sandringham. Knowing of the Queen's affection for the little watch—the dial of which measured only three-sixteenths of an inch across—the most intensive search went on for it over many weeks, but it was never recovered. It was a charming gesture on the part of the French people to have another 'just like it' presented to Her Majesty on her state visit to France in 1957. Destined as a surprise gift, the news leaked out but did not spoil the manifest pleasure which the replica gift gave the Queen.

It was not until she reached the age of twenty-one in 1947 that the Queen received her first gift of really important jewels. At that time she was, with her father and mother and Princess Margaret, on a tour of South Africa. What more natural, then, that the Union of South Africa, home of the world's loveliest diamonds, should mark the event by a gift of some of the Union's finest gems? Certainly it must have been one of the most magnificent twenty-first birthday gifts anyone has ever received—a collection of twenty-one large, flawless diamonds plus one, of equally unmatched 'fire' and purity, from the De Beers Corporation. Specially selected from an immense pile of 'rough' these splendid diamonds varied in size up to ten carats. Cut and polished in Johannesburg, they were presented to the then Princess Elizabeth to set to her own wishes as a necklace. Later Her Majesty, who had had them first in the form of a matinée-length necklace, decided to have it of a shorter length and the diamonds that were accordingly left over were mounted as a matching bracelet, completely simple in design but utterly magnificent by reason of the unparalleled quality of the diamonds. Small wonder that the Queen refers to them as 'my best diamonds'—a view which has been appreciated by those who have had the opportunity of seeing these jewels at close quarters, numbering many, for she has been most generous in lending them for exhibitions held in aid of charity. As her first gift of important jewellery they probably hold a special place in her esteem.

They were, however, but a foretaste of the breathtakingly beautiful jewels that were to come into her possession with her marriage in November of that same year to the Duke of Edinburgh. From her grandmother, the late Queen Mary, the Queen received no fewer than nine splendid gifts of jewellery, among them the all-diamond tiara (her first), affectionately described by Her Majesty as 'Grannie's tiara'. This had been given to Queen Mary on her own marriage in 1893 by the Girls of Great Britain and Ireland. It is very light in weight and appearance, with its delicate scroll and collet design and diamond points. Another wonderful wedding gift from Queen Mary was a diamond stomacher quite eight inches in length which the Queen can wear as a whole but of which she prefers to wear the smallest portion.

Queen Mary had already taught her royal grandchild a great deal about the history and art of jewellery and its place and importance in the royal scene—a lesson which Queen Elizabeth II no doubt found gave her an added appreciation for these gifts.

Her parents' wedding gifts were equally notable and, like those from Queen Mary, have been worn frequently by the Queen during her reign. Among the necklaces is a 'bandeau' of gold set with rubies and diamonds which she frequently wears. King George VI also gave her a beautiful mid-nineteenth-century necklace of rectangular sapphires, each one framed in diamonds, with a large diamond between each one and with drop ear-rings *en suite*, each with a large rectangular sapphire framed with diamonds. These are a great favourite of the Queen's. The necklace is really a necklet, because it comes just below the base of the throat in length.

The Queen's personal wedding gift from her bridegroom was a broad bracelet of diamonds, but her innately simple taste in jewellery is best exemplified in her engagement ring, the central diamond of which is a three-carat diamond flanked by five smaller diamonds on each side, made up from a family ring which had belonged to Prince Philip's mother, Princess Andrew of Greece. Her wedding ring, made of Welsh gold, is just a plain, rather narrow, gold band.

Magnificence was the keynote, however, of most of the jewels which the Queen received as a bride from people outside the Royal Family. From the City of London came a handsome early-nineteenth-century fringed necklace of diamonds and from the Nizam of Hyderabad a tiara of massed diamonds with a three-dimensional flower design (the flowers of which are detachable to be worn as separate jewels) and a matching necklace.

One of the loveliest of the many lovely gifts given to Queen Elizabeth II on her coronation was the necklace and brooch of aquamarines and diamonds from the President and people of Brazil which she first wore—to the admiration of all who saw the jewels on that occasion—at the gala performance at Covent

Garden Opera House in 1954 for the King and Queen of Sweden's state visit. These two jewels were augmented, in 1958, by a further gift from the President and the peoples of Brazil of an aquamarine and diamond bracelet and dress clip. Sources of aquamarines in Brazil are very low and it took a whole year to find exactly matching stones to go with the necklace and brooch. To make the gift even more precious, hundreds of diamonds were used in the form of clusters like small crowns. According to the Brazilian Ambassador to London, Senhor Assis de Chateaubriand, who made the presentation, 'the Queen adored the gift' and told him she had acquired an aquamarine tiara—and had had the Brazilian necklace shortened, without, however, omitting any of the stones in the process showing that here again Her Majesty had preferred a shorter-length necklace.

Another outstanding gift to the Queen was the world's most perfect rose-pink diamond which was a present from the late Dr J. N. Williamson and was found in his diamond mines in Tanganyika. Quite flawless, unmatched in the perfection of its colour, this priceless diamond was found in 1941 in the Mwadui mine and was given as a wedding gift. It was not, however, until the year of her Coronation in 1953 that the Queen finally decided how it should be set. Weighing 54 carats when it was found and 23·6 carats when it was finally cut to perfection, she had the diamond set in the centre of a flower spray brooch, jonquil-shaped, with curved petals of navette-cut diamonds, the flower on a stem of baguette diamonds, with two large navette-cut diamonds, one on each side of the stalk, to represent 'leaves'. The brooch measures $4\frac{1}{2}$ inches from tip to tip and the Queen frequently wears it as a lapel brooch at formal daytime functions for which it is admirably 'right' and royal.

Though naturally no one outside the Court knows with any preciseness exactly the extent of the Queen's collection of personal jewellery, most of her subjects know from observation that she now has several magnificent tiaras, yet for her marriage in 1947 the then Princess Elizabeth chose, as 'something borrowed', her mother's fringed Russian-style tiara composed of vertical rows of diamonds graduating from a high point in the centre front to a narrow band at the back. Since that time Her Majesty has acquired by gift, and by inheritance from Queen Mary, the beautiful tiara of entwined ovals of diamonds with fifteen large pendeloque pearls hanging from the centre of each oval which are interchangeable with fifteen *cabochon* drop emeralds of great beauty. The tiara was a gift from the Grand Duchess Vladimir of Russia and it was Queen Mary's idea to have the fifteen drop emeralds to substitute, as desired, for the drop pearls of the original. To go with this tiara there is a particularly fine necklace in circlet form composed of *cabochon* emeralds surrounded by diamonds, held between a double row of diamonds with a single large diamond between each diamond-set emerald, while from the front, suspended from two single lines of diamonds, hang one superb pear-shaped *cabochon* emerald and a single marquise diamond cut from the Cullinan diamond. The pear-shaped emeralds in the tiara and those in the necklet and brooch which complete the parure had been presented by Augusta, Duchess of Cambridge, to Princess Mary, Duchess of Teck, the mother of Queen Mary. Originally they had been won in a lottery in Frankfurt in the nineteenth century.

Like these, inherited from Queen Mary, is the two-stone brooch of great beauty composed of a single square diamond from which hangs a single pear-shaped diamond—the third and fourth portions of the Cullinan, the largest diamond ever mined. This huge stone, which weighed $1\frac{1}{2}$ lb. when found and was the size of a man's fist, came from the Premier Mine in Kimberley in 1905 and was presented to King Edward VII by the Transvaal Government at the instigation of General Smuts and General Botha on the King's birthday in 1907. From the hundred and more stones which were cut from the great diamond (named by King Edward the 'Star of Africa'), the largest and most spectacular portion is set in the head of the Sceptre and the next largest in the front of the Imperial State Crown. This can be worn as a brooch and both Queen Alexandra and Queen Mary wore this dazzlingly beautiful diamond on several state occasions, the last time Queen

Bird and flower brooches for day and early evening wear by Garrard & Company, Ltd., London. They are mainly made up of diamonds, rubies, gold and platinum.

Also by Garrard, these birds and flowers are emblems of the states. The eagle, our national bird, is made of 18-carat gold set with topaz and emeralds. In the centre is a poodle with a difference by Cartier. The ears flap, the head turns, and the curls are pearls. These jewels were all shown in the British Exhibition in New York, 1960.

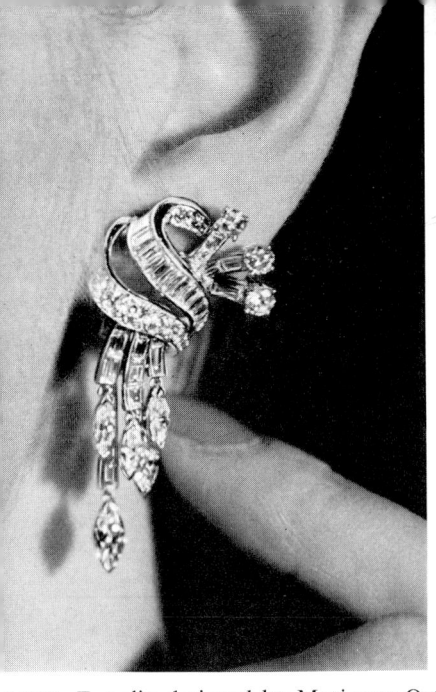

LEFT: Ear-clip designed by Marianne Ostier of New York. RIGHT: A pear-shaped diamond falls from a diamond spray; by Julius Cohen of New York.

LEFT: "Red, white and diamonds" by Schimpff Studio of Bloomington, Illinois. A panel of red enamel, a single pearl, and a curve of diamonds. RIGHT: Diamond and ruby flowers, worn as dress or hair ornament, by Garrard.

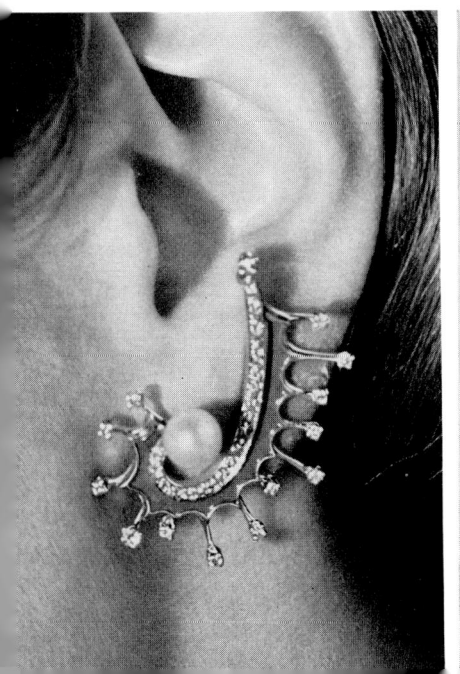

From reed to ring—a short history of the betrothal symbol:
1. Plaited grass or rushes; earliest known type of troth ring.
2. Thong of leather as improvised by Roman soldiers in Europe.
3. Colonial diamond hoop, called a "keeper" ring. It was placed next to wedding band to keep the band from being lost.
4. Bouquet cluster of large diamonds; nineteenth century. Silver top to give diamonds white reflections, gold band around finger.
5. Our grandmother's engagement ring, half-hoop with six matched diamonds in a row.
6. Diamond solitaire in Tiffany prong setting, the classic engagement ring from about 1890.

Mary so wore it being at the wedding of the present Queen in 1947.

Having borrowed her mother's sunray tiara for her wedding, Queen Elizabeth II subsequently became possessed of one of her own when Queen Mary bequeathed to her the Russian fringe tiara which had been given to Queen Alexandra by her friends on her silver wedding in 1888. It was worn for the first time by the present Queen when, in full state robes, she opened Parliament in Wellington, New Zealand, in 1954.

Another tiara with special interest which the Queen inherited from her grandmother is the pearl one with nineteen pendeloque pearls which Queen Mary had had specially made up from various ornaments. It is a charming jewel, the pearls suspended from graceful diamond bow motifs, each surmounted by a single diamond. In addition to the nineteen pendeloque pearls, inverted drop pearls can be worn between these diamond points—another example of Queen Mary's liking for 'interchangeable' jewels.

An opal of more than 200 carats—the Andamooka opal—is a striking feature of the opal and diamond necklace with matching ear-rings which was presented to the Queen by the Government of Southern Australia in 1954. The Andamooka is one of the finest and biggest white opals ever found in Australia. There are nearly two hundred fine diamonds in the necklace centred by the opal, and in the ear-rings.

The splendid looped necklace of pearls and diamonds which the Queen generally wears at gala performances at the theatre is one which was presented to Princess Alexandra on the occasion of her wedding to the Prince of Wales in 1863 by King Frederick VII of Denmark. At that time it had the pendant Cross of Dagmar suspended from it, but the Queen wears the necklace without the pendant—again demonstrating her preference for necklaces of short length.

Having begun to wear ear-rings at the age of eighteen, it was not until 1951, just before the royal visit to Canada, that the Queen was prevailed upon to have her ears pierced in order to be able to wear her impressive chandelier ear-rings of large diamonds, the wedding gift of her parents, so suited to state occasions and visits. The weight of these made ear-piercing imperative if they were to be secure; hitherto the Queen had preferred to wear simple pearl studs or small diamond clusters as ear clips. Once the ear-piercing was accomplished she was able to delight her subjects by wearing much more splendid ear-rings, among them the superb pendeloque pearl drop ear-rings which were a wedding gift from the Sheik of Bahrein.

The Queen's collection of brooches must be unique. Apart from family jewels very many brooches and dress clips have been given to her from time to time from public bodies, regiments, civic heads and others. Her first gift of this kind was when, on her sixteenth birthday, she was presented as Colonel-in-Chief with a badge of the Grenadier Guards in diamonds, sapphires and enamel. Among the most beautiful is the brooch in diamonds in the form of the flame lily which is the emblem flower of Southern Rhodesia and which was presented to her on the occasion of the royal visit in 1947. For the making of this faithful replica in diamonds of a living flower a bloom was specially flown to South Africa and the artist worked against time to complete his drawing of it before the flower faded. All the children of Southern Rhodesia contributed their pennies to this exquisite gift, one of which the Queen seems especially fond and which she usually wears when visiting children's schools and hospitals. Another favourite of hers, so the Queen Mother is reported to have said, is the spray brooch in the form of a wattle flower given to her during her Australian tour in 1954. This is made entirely of yellow diamonds to represent the wattle (mimosa) blossom and the gathering together of the matched yellow diamonds of which is is composed presented a problem —many of the stones had to be secured from private sources.

Most of the commemorative brooches given to the Queen have interesting features which make them unique in every way. There is the brooch made of Leadhills gold mined locally which was given to her in October 1956. The centre of the brooch is in the form of a heart, surrounded by a circular gem-set border of thistles and leaves. The Leadhill gold mines in Lanarkshire were once quite rich and it is even today a popular weekend pastime among visitors to search there for gold. In fact, some of the local gold in the Queen's brooch was given by a businessman who had collected it on his holidays in Leadhill. Another brooch which was presented to the Queen when she opened the new Queen's Bridge over the Tay at Perth in October 1960, was in the form of a miniature flower bouquet with amethyst buds surrounded with ferns and grasses with a central group of mauve-tinted pearls found in the Scottish river which flows beneath the bridge.

Of her family gifts the Queen almost always wears with the Ribbon of the Order of the Garter, securing it on the shoulder, a large diamond bow brooch in a 'true lover's knot' design which was a gift from Queen Mary, who gave similar brooches to Princess Margaret and the Duchess of Kent. Her Majesty on these occasions wears also the Family Orders—diamond-encircled hand-painted miniatures of her father and grandfather, suspended from a ribbon bow. These were instituted by George I in the form of a cameo. Later, in King Edward VII's reign, miniatures of the Sovereign replaced the cameo. Those the Queen wears are of her father, King George VI, and her grandfather, King George V, and are mounted on a pale pink and pale blue bow respectively. Those she has bestowed on the ladies of her immediate family have her own portrait in miniature mounted on a pale yellow moiré silk ribbon bow.

One brooch which always excites admiration is a diamond-set corsage jewel from which hang three large pear-shaped pearls which was a gift from Queen Mary and which the Queen frequently wears with the handsome triple-row pearl necklace which was a gift from the Sheik of Qatar.

The flashing diamond and pearl diadem of crosses patée and floral emblems of the United Kingdom which the Queen wears on her journey to open a new Parliament was designed by George IV and was worn on a similar occasion in 1837 by Queen Victoria. Surprisingly, the Queen seems to wear only two rings

—her engagement ring of diamonds, and the plain circlet of her wedding ring made from a piece of gold mined in North Wales.

Like the Queen, Queen Elizabeth the Queen Mother has a wonderful collection of jewels, many of them family ones, but the greater number are official gifts which have been made to her from time to time. It has been said that rubies are her favourite gem and this certainly seems to be borne out by the story of the beautiful flower spray brooch which was presented to her by the people of Australia on her visit to the Commonwealth. The brooch, which is a three-dimensional replica of the Australian hibiscus flower and measures $3\frac{1}{2}$ inches in length, contains 346 flawless South African diamonds encrusting the leaves and petals with thirty-four fine-quality Burma rubies forming the throats and stamens of the flowers, the whole set in platinum. Originally these central stones were planned to be two Lightning Ridge opals, indigenous to Australia. The Australian Prime Minister's Secretary, Sir Allen Brown, was instructed, when he visited London to finalize arrangements for the royal tour, to sound the Queen Mother on her preference in gems. A code cable was arranged, 'Opals in' or, alternatively, 'Opals out'. In due course the cable was despatched—'Opals out'. On his return to Australia Sir Allen said he had discovered that the Queen Mother's favourite gem is the ruby. When Her Majesty duly received the ruby and diamond brooch in Canberra she looked at it a long time, murmuring, 'How beautiful, how very beautiful.' Unpinning the brooch she was wearing, she replaced it by the new one, lifting it up from time to time to gaze at it admiringly.

The Queen Mother also has a parure consisting of a cluster necklace and tiara of rubies and diamonds and ruby and diamond ear-rings *en suite* which are family heirlooms and which are believed to have been designed by Prince Albert. The glowing rich red of rubies is particularly becoming to Her Majesty's colouring. The Queen Mother also likes, it would seem, the alliance of pearls and diamonds for evening wear, for her famous four-row pearl necklace is often partnered by a striking pearl and diamond lapel brooch which is one of her earliest pieces of jewellery. Like the Queen, the Queen Mother received many gifts of beautiful jewels from Queen Mary, among them the unusual tiara shaped in a broad curving band with a large central sapphire. Another gift from Queen Mary was a handsome and quite large floral spray set entirely with diamonds. A particularly fine diamond brooch in the form of a single feather which she sometimes wears was a private gift from a friend, while the striking diamond tiara in an unusual trellis design which has been much remarked upon by observers was left to her by another friend.

When she visited South Africa in 1947, with the late King George VI and the two Princesses, the Queen Mother was given a lovely unset marquise diamond of 8·55 carats contained in a gold casket, and the King a gift of 399 diamonds to form a Garter Star. This was subsequently made and is an outstandingly fine jewel.

All the ladies of the Royal Family show a charming felicity in choosing jewels appropriate to the occasion, as, for example, when the Queen Mother visited Canada she wore (as did the Queen on her visit there) a pair of diamond-set maple leaf brooches. When she visits Scotland the Queen Mother usually wears a handsome diamond brooch in the form of thistle heads and leaves. An unobtrusively gracious act was the pinning of an enamelled badge of the Cross of Lorraine to her white evening bag when the Queen Mother attended a state banquet at the French Embassy. And, of course, whenever they visit the regiments of which they are Colonels-in-Chief the royal ladies invariably wear pinned to their lapel a jewelled replica of the regiment's badge. The Queen Mother appears to like, on private occasions, to wear the beautiful sapphire and diamond flower brooch which was an anniversary gift from King George VI. This matched her sapphire and diamond engagement ring, which had to be made specially to fit the Queen Mother's very small finger.

Princess Margaret has a larger collection of jewels than one would suppose from her public appearances for she was left a number of really beautiful and historically interesting jewels by her grandmother, Queen Mary, though her jewels are not extensive compared with those of Queen Elizabeth II and the Queen Mother. Perhaps her very first 'jewel' was the simple little necklet of pink coral which she wore at the age of three. Her grandfather, King George V, gave her her first 'grown-up' necklace—a double row of fine pearls—when she was a young girl and this was practically the only jewellery she wore until quite late in her teens. The Princess has never had her ears pierced, for with her infallible taste for what she considered appropriate to her height she appears to scale her jewels, seldom wearing the very long chandelier type of ear-ring which would necessitate having her ears pierced. Those drop ear-rings which she does wear—usually pear-shaped pearls between two rows of diamonds hanging from a single diamond—are of moderate length and weight. Perhaps the longest chandelier ear-rings which Princess Margaret wears are those in diamonds which were presented to her in December 1958 to commemorate her launching of the *Otago* at Southampton. When presented with them the Princess exclaimed, 'How absolutely lovely! I am going to wear them tonight.' This she did at a theatre visit that evening to see *West Side Story*. She was also presented with a diamond necklace by the shipbuilders and a golden eagle emblem brooch by the owners of the vessel.

Like her royal mother and sister, the Princess has been the recipient of many official gifts of jewellery, principally brooches and clips. One of the handsome diamond flower brooches in this category is the rose spray brooch which she received as a commemorative gift from Vickers Armstrong. In August 1958 she received a diamond-studded gold maple leaf and beaver brooch with matching ear-rings from the Mayor of Ottawa. The previous month the Princess had been given a brooch in the form of a six-petalled dogwood flower set with 239 diamonds, the stamens outlined in brown diamonds and the leaves set with emeralds, presented by the Premier of British Columbia—a truly beautiful jewel.

When the Princess launched the *Carinthia*, the Cunard Company and John Brown Limited jointly presented her with a diamond spray brooch of early-nineteenth-century design with a large central diamond in a flower motif, with leaves and stalks of gold and silver, diamond-set. During her visit to Rhodesia Princess Margaret received a diamond brooch in a replica of the Rhodesian flame lily, like that which the Queen had been given. While on her highly enjoyed and successful trip to the Caribbean the Princess was presented with a nutmeg brooch of great charm, in gold enamelled in red and brown in the shape of a ripe, bursting nutmeg on a stem bearing two leaves. For that Caribbean tour the Princess followed a course more usual in less exalted families and borrowed some of the jewellery she took with her. Of the four tiaras which she wore on several state and formal occasions only one was her own—the light and delicate scroll circlet with fan-shaped motifs set in diamonds. The broad curved band of diamonds with a central large sapphire was loaned by the Queen Mother, as was a third tiara with inverted diamond festoons and pearl spikes which the Queen Mother had worn at her own wedding in 1923, but as a bandeau securing her veil low on the forehead as was the fashion in the 'twenties.

The wonderful high diamond tiara which Princess Margaret wore so beautifully and effectively at her wedding was one of her own private purchases. This was bought at a public sale at Sotheby's on the Princess's behalf and was sold by Lord Poltimore whose daughter, Lady Stucley, had found it too heavy to wear. The tiara can be taken to pieces to form a magnificent necklace (in which guise the Princess has most often worn it since her marriage) or as a smaller circlet for the hair. For the necklace version the seven vertical sprays in the tiara are worn, bib-fashion, suspended from the base of the tiara which forms the actual necklace of choker length.

In November of 1957 the late Dr John Williamson presented the Princess with a wonderful dahlia brooch containing some of the finest diamonds from his mines in Tanganyika—a massive piece which measures 4 inches in length by 3½ inches in width. Its size is probably the reason why one seldom sees the Princess wearing this brooch.

Some of the Princess's first family gifts of jewellery came from her father, King George VI, who had some of the rather heavy ancestral jewellery reset in modern, lighter form and in 1951 at Balmoral presented them to the Princess on her twenty-first birthday. One of her favourites of these jewels, it is believed, is a diamond brooch in the form of an ear of corn of late Victorian design of about 1880. The Queen Mother also gave the Princess a parure of turquoises and diamonds which had been a wedding gift from the late King and which the Princess had slightly remodelled, while retaining the antique style of the design. This parure is admirably suited to the Princess's colouring and she wears it often.

A favourite necklace and one in which she is most frequently seen is a choker necklace of collet diamonds from which the Princess sometimes wears a pear-shaped pearl in the centre front with drop pearl ear-rings *en suite*. Queen Mary gave the Princess, among many other wonderful jewels, a bracelet in pearls, diamonds and sapphires while her father gave her a wider one set entirely with diamonds. Since her marriage the Princess has been seen wearing a very long spray of diamond-set flowers, three blossoms set one above the other. This she has worn on the lapel of a tweed suit on a visit to Balmoral, and on the shoulder of an evening gown at the theatre—and it looked equally 'right' on both widely diverse occasions.

Princess Margaret is highly individual in her choice and use of jewels and has unconsciously been a trend-setter—perhaps because of this. When she wore two small diamond brooches set at spaced intervals on the crown of a small hat women were quick to follow the royal example. Another fashion was the wearing of a matching pair of clips, one in the hat and the other on the lapel of the coat, in the Princess's case two heart-shaped clips set with diamonds. She also revived a fashion set by Queen Victoria by wearing a flexible gold bracelet twined round her arm in the form of a serpent and this, too, set women searching for these Victorian bracelets.

Whatever Princess Margaret wears in the way of jewellery is manifestly chosen with care and is always beautifully in proportion. With so much from which to choose from her personal jewels her fastidious selectivity is a matter of admiration to students of fashions and their accessories. Whereas the Queen wears her jewels, on formal occasions only, as a regal and necessary appendage to her exalted position, Princess Margaret is freer to follow her own dictates. What emerges from a survey of the treasury of royal jewels is, firstly, how magnificently they underline the special power and might of the Throne, and secondly, how little jewellery the royal ladies wear in their private lives, and how fundamentally simple are their personal tastes.

CHAPTER ELEVEN

The Crown Jewels of England

PERHAPS the most famous collection of jewels in the world —apart from personally owned royal gems—is that which comprises the Crown Jewels of England. The impressive coronation ceremony would lose much of its splendour without its jewelled regalia and richly coloured robes. These symbols of kingship, of equity and justice, of spirituality and mercy, are indeed a stimulating and beautiful sight, while to describe the wealth of history and tradition behind the Crown Jewels of England is to open wide the pages of history, for the original Crown Regalia can be traced back to the year A.D. 853 and the reign of Aethelwulf, when the young Prince Alfred was sent to Rome to receive the Papal Blessing and the Crown.

Though intrinsically valued by some at somewhere around £20,000,000 the Crown Jewels are really priceless, for much of their true value lies in their symbolism and historical interest. To British people throughout the world the Regalia provide a link between the present day and the Britain of more than a thousand years ago. Had it not been for the vandalism of Cromwell's Commonwealth Government which decided in 1649 to melt down or sell all symbols of monarchy, the Regalia would still contain the crown worn by Alfred the Great when he was crowned the first King of a Unified England at Winchester in A.D. 871, though visitors can still see in the Jewel House of the Tower of London the jewels actually worn or handled by Edward the Confessor, the Black Prince, and the first Queen Elizabeth.

For more than 700 years the Crown Jewels have reposed in the Tower of London, but before that they were kept in the Abbey Church of Westminster, where they were not particularly well protected so that many depredations were made upon them under the careless custodianship. When James II came to the throne he found the Crown of England was so battered, and so many gems had been pilfered from it to be replaced by imitation gems, that the repair and replacements cost £12,000. An attempt to rob the Royal Treasury in 1303 led to its removal from the Abbey, and by the time Henry III ascended the throne some of the King's jewels had already been moved to the White Tower. When what was brought from the Abbey was added to this, the collection was found to be so extensive that it was decided to build a special Jewel House to contain it. Here the King's treasure was kept in comparative safety—comparative because it was still occasionally despoiled in order to raise money for war-making. It was usual, in the Middle Ages, for kings throughout Europe to accumulate wealth in the form of jewels and plate as a reserve 'fund' to draw upon when a war had to be financed.

But these depredations were as nothing compared with the vandalism of the Commonwealth Government in ordering all the insignia of British Royalty to be sold, melted down, or destroyed. It gained only a few hundred pounds for Cromwell but it lost posterity the priceless symbols of royalty. King Alfred the Great's crown of 'gould wyerworke set with slight stones and two little bells' fetched only £248 10*s*, while poor Queen Edith's little crown only realized £16. There is a legend that the ancient Crown of England still exists; that it was secreted by some Royalist and its hiding place never revealed.

Fortunately some of the Regalia did escape the pillage of 1649, notably the Gold Ampulla or Sacred Eagle, which held the anointing oil, and the Anointing Spoon. Several of the famous gems with centuries of history behind them were also recovered and now occupy prominent positions in the royal crowns. Among these gems is the sapphire which was set into the Coronation Ring of Edward the Confessor; the pearl ear-rings worn by Queen Elizabeth I, and the famous Black Prince's ruby (actually a spinel, though it is recorded as a ruby). These are all set in the Imperial State Crown. The Black Prince's ruby, which looks like a large clot of congealed blood, is about two inches long and one and a half inches wide and has been variously valued as worth from £100,000 to £150,000. Its history is bound up in bloodshed and murder, but it remains one of the most interesting and admired gems in existence. It was first heard of in 1369, when it was already many centuries old. It was at that time owned by the King of Granada who was murdered by Don Pedro of Castille (Peter the Cruel) who coveted the gem. He in turn gave it to the Black Prince as a token of gratitude for his assistance on the battlefield of Navarette, when English soldiers under the command of Edward III's famous son rendered the Spanish king invaluable help.

On the death of the Black Prince the ruby passed into the possession of his son, Richard II, but it soon figured again in battle, this time at Agincourt in 1415, when Henry V rode into the fray wearing the ruby in his coronet. Seventy years later, in 1485, Richard III wore it at the Battle of Bosworth Field. Richard was killed and the Crown, which had been hastily but ineffectually hidden in a hawthorn bush, was retrieved and used to crown on the spot the first of the Tudors—Henry VII. The last dramatic adventure to befall the ruby was its attempted theft from the Tower of London by the notorious Captain Blood. It was said to have been in his pocket when he was captured. His 'punishment' provides a fascinating field of speculation, for far from being beheaded or given some other condign punishment for his daring robbery, it is said that the notorious captain was given an annuity. And this in the days when a man could be—and was—hanged for stealing a sheep. From its replacement at that time in the Royal Crown the ruby remained in its accustomed setting until Cromwell swept the Regalia into the melting pot and the market. His inventory contemptuously described the ruby as 'a large ballas ruby, pierced and wraped in paper, value £4'—for which sum it was sold. Fortunately the gem was recovered many years later and ever since the Restoration it has been set in the front of the State Crown.

Even older than the Black Prince's ruby is the St Edward's sapphire set at the top of the Crown, for this was originally set in the Coronation Ring worn by Edward the Confessor at his crowning in 1042. It remained buried with him in Westminster Abbey until 1101, when the shrine was broken open and this and other jewels removed.

The Stuart sapphire, which Charles II had set in the front of the State Crown during the Restoration, and which is now set in the back, also has a romantic history. James II took it to France with him when he was dethroned and for a hundred years it remained a Stuart possession. Eventually Cardinal York, who had inherited it, bequeathed the sapphire to George III in 1807 and it was presented by him to his grand-daughter Charlotte (d. 1817). After the deaths of both Charlotte and George III, the jewel was recognized by George IV in 1821. The King was able eventually to buy back the gem, though no details of the transaction, nor of the price paid, were ever published. On her accession, Queen Victoria had the sapphire set in the Royal Crown below the ruby and there it remained until it was reset at the back of the Crown to make way for the Second Star of Africa—the second largest diamond in the world at that time. This was mounted so that it could be removed for wearing as a brooch by the reigning queen on state occasions, as it is frequently worn.

Probably the most interesting of the State Jewels is the Imperial State Crown because of the richness of its appearance, the beauty of its gems, and the wealth of history associated with them. The form of the Crown has been altered from time to time but the same jewels have been used again and again. The present Crown was made for Queen Victoria in its present form in 1838. It has two complete arches which pass from front to back and from side to side, with the central orb on the top surmounted by a jewelled cross. The wide, jewelled band which forms the base of the Crown has in its centre the Second Star of Africa, cut from the great Cullinan diamond. Above this jewelled band are alternating gem-studded crosses and fleur-de-lis. The central cross above the Second Star of Africa diamond has as its central gem the Black Prince's ruby. At the point of intersection of the two arches on top of the Crown hang four large pearls—the Queen Elizabeth I pearls. In the jewelled cross surmounting the orb is set Edward the Confessor's sapphire, and at the back is another large sapphire which once adorned the crown of Charles II. In all, the Imperial State Crown contains 2,783 diamonds, 277 pearls (one a Welsh river pearl found in the River Conway and given by Sir Richard Wynn), 17 sapphires, 11 emeralds and 5 rubies.

The Imperial Crown of India is another magnificent piece, heavily encrusted with rich gems. It was specially made for the visit of King George V to India in 1912, when he was acclaimed Emperor. It had been intended to use the Imperial State Crown but it was discovered that the laws of England forbade its being taken out of the country, hence the necessity for making an entirely new one—a redundant, if beautiful, item in the Royal Regalia since the Monarch is no longer 'Emperor of India'. The Imperial Crown of India, like the Imperial State Crown, has a jewelled headband with alternating crosses and fleurs-de-lis, but there are eight half-arches curving up to the centrepiece, instead of the usual two full arches. These half-arches are richly ornamented with diamonds and each is decorated with a diamond-set lotus flower, while both the orb and cross surmounting the Crown are diamond-set. In all, the Crown contains 6,170 diamonds, 4 sapphires, 4 rubies and 6 remarkably fine emeralds. One of these, a magnificent gem weighing 34 carats, cut *en cabochon*, is set in the centre of the jewelled band in front.

The Coronation Crown, with which the Monarch is actually crowned, is called St Edward's Crown. This is not, as its name would imply, the Crown which was used at the coronation of Edward the Confessor, for that was seized and destroyed by the Roundheads. The present St Edward's Crown was made in 1662 for Charles II and is of gold, set with diamonds, rubies, sapphires, emeralds and pearls. Above the band are alternating crosses and fleur-de-lis and over these stretch the two complete arches symbolizing the Heredity and Independence of the Monarchy. The arches curve downwards in the centre to symbolize Royalty, whereas on the Imperial Crowns the arches maintain their upward curve—an emblem of imperial power.

Decorating the edges of the arches on the St Edward's Crown

are rows of pearls, while large drop pearls hang from the crossbar of the gold and gem-studded cross surmounting the orb on the top. The Crown itself is very heavy—it weighs nearly 5 lb.—and for this reason it rests upon the head of the Sovereign for but a few moments at the coronation ceremony before being exchanged for the lighter Imperial Crown of State. Every Sovereign since Charles II has been actually crowned with the St Edward's Crown with the exception of Queen Victoria, for whom it was considered to be too heavy. Instead she was crowned with the Imperial State Crown which was specially remade for her coronation. Even so, tradition was not to be denied, and as it was felt that no coronation would be complete without the St Edward's Crown it was carried throughout the ceremony by the Lord High Steward.

These are the three most important crowns in the Regalia, but the collection includes some very beautiful crowns and diadems made for Queens Consort. Queen Mary's Crown, set entirely with wonderful diamonds, which is used at the coronation ceremony was Her Majesty's private property. In it are set the famous Koh-i-Noor diamond and the two lesser 'Stars of Africa' cut from the Cullinan diamond. These three stones are set in such a way that they can be removed and worn separately as pendant and brooch. The Koh-i-Noor was presented to Queen Victoria by the East India Company at the time of the annexation of the Punjab and it is thought that the diamond originally weighed more than 1,000 carats. Before coming into the possession of the Crown the stone (described in earlier records as an uncut but highly polished diamond) passed through many hands and was recut from time to time, not always by scrupulously honest cutters. It weighed only 186 carats when it was presented to Queen Victoria and further recutting reduced the diamond to its present size of 106 carats. Queen Victoria, however, never wore the Koh-i-Noor in her crown but as a brooch, and Queen Mary, Consort of King George V, was the first queen to have the stone set in her crown.

Next in importance to the crowns as emblems of Sovereignty

are the Orb and Sceptres. The Orb, surmounted by the Cross, symbolizes the domination of the Christian Faith over the world. The Orb is never placed in the hands of a consort but only of a reigning king or queen. The King's Orb is a ball of pure gold, richly girdled with a pearl-bordered fillet, inside which are set large rubies, sapphires and emeralds surrounded by diamonds, while a similar jewelled band passes over the top half of the Orb. The surmounting Cross is separated from the Orb by a very fine large amethyst and the Cross itself is heavily jewelled with a fine sapphire occupying the centre front and an equally fine emerald the back. The arms of the Cross are studded with diamonds and pearls.

The Queen's Orb has been used on only one occasion—the coronation of William and Mary, for which ceremony it was specially made. It is very similar to the King's Orb but is slightly smaller in size and does not have the large amethyst between the golden globe and the Cross.

There are five sceptres in the Crown Regalia. The Royal Sceptre with the Cross is a symbol of kingly power and justice and is held in the Monarch's right hand at the coronation. Made for Charles II, it has been altered from time to time and is about three feet in length, of gold richly studded with gems. At the top of the Sceptre is the Orb cut out of a large amethyst, richly girdled with diamonds and rubies and surmounted by a magnificent diamond-studded cross with a fine central emerald. The Orb and Cross both stand on the largest cut diamond in the world—the Great Star of Africa, the pear-shaped brilliant cut from the Cullinan diamond. This enormous stone weighs $516\frac{1}{2}$ carats and is quite flawless. It is held in place in the Sceptre by two hinged clasps in such a way that it can be removed and worn by the Queen as a pendant on great state occasions.

The King's Sceptre with the Dove is held in the left hand of the Sovereign and is a symbol of equity and mercy. This Sceptre, too, is of gold surmounted by an orb of gold with diamond-studded girdle, and a golden cross upon which stands a white enamelled dove with outstretched wings. The staff of the Sceptre is richly enamelled and jewelled. A second Sceptre with Dove was made for the Queen at the coronation of William and Mary but has not since been used.

The Queen's Sceptre with the Cross, which is held in the Queen's right hand (when the Queen is a consort and not a monarch) after she has been crowned, is of gold and diamonds. It measures about two feet ten inches in length and at the top has a double *fleur-de-lis*, diamond-set, holding a golden orb with diamond-set girdle and arch surmounted in turn by a diamond-set cross. In the Queen Consort's left hand is placed the Queen's Ivory Rod, three and a half feet in length, consisting of pieces of ivory joined together with bands of gold. At the top is a golden orb, richly enamelled, surmounted by a cross on which rests a dove with closed wings.

Of the five Swords of State the one of the greatest intrinsic worth is the Jewelled State Sword, the scabbard of which is thickly set with gems—diamonds, rubies and emeralds being used to depict the Rose of England, the Thistle of Scotland and the Shamrock of Ireland. At the bottom of the scabbard is a fine turquoise set around with diamonds, while the hilt is richly jewelled and has a particularly fine diamond set at the top.

Mention should be made of one more jewel—the Coronation Ring, sometimes known as the Wedding Ring of England. This ring is made for each sovereign and becomes his or her private property on the coronation. Those of Queen Victoria and King George V may be seen in the collection of Crown Jewels at the Tower of London. Both rings consist of a sapphire set around with diamonds, with a St George's Cross in rubies superimposed.

The British Crown Jewels in the Jewel House at the Tower of London are protected by an armour-plate treasury, which takes the form of an octagon measuring about sixteen feet across—a small area in which to contain the most famous collection of jewels in the world.

CHAPTER TWELVE

Birthstones

PERHAPS the most completely personal aspect of jewellery is provided by the range of gemstones which constitute the birthstone for each of the twelve Zodiacal periods of the year. The birthstone had its origin in ancient lore concerning gemstones and each known gem had its attributed powers, a relation being found between certain gems and certain astrological periods. There has been in the past much dispute as to which is the right gem for each period; in ancient times, and in fact until recent years, stones were named and judged by their colour and this was the deciding factor in making a certain stone appropriate for a given month.

The belief in the mystical properties of gemstones raised many divergencies of opinion which were finally resolved in 1912 by the American Retail Jewellers' Association, which drew up an official list which is now accepted as the correct one. This was qualified, in 1938, by the American Gemological Society—a group of people dealing mostly in gems.

Doubt was also created by the difference between the Zodiacal month and the calendar month. Adapting each birthstone to a calendar month is perhaps a facile way, but it is not astrologically accurate. Long before the Roman calendar was arrived at, gems had been assigned to a part of the Zodiac. Division of the year for this is based on the equinoxes when the sun enters Aries (28th March) or Libra (23rd September). The heavens were mapped out with constellations symbolized by mythological figures and animals; those in the belt along which the Sun made its yearly course were called the Zodiac, with signs for each period such as waves for Aquarius, twins for Gemini and so on. Records show that from the earliest times these signs were engraved or used as jewellery designs for persons born in the different Zodiacal period.

Of these twelve Zodiacal periods the first may be accepted to be Aquarius, the sign governing those born from 20th January to 18th February, for whom the birthstone is the garnet. This is a gem that has been treasured for centuries and which was valued as a talisman by the ancient Egyptians. They used to engrave garnets with cabalistic symbols to increase their powers. In India and in Persia the garnet was used as an amulet against risk of poisoning and the plague and it was also considered to be effective as a protection against lightning. In the Middle Ages —a time when medical properties were attributed to gemstones— it was thought to be a remedy against inflammatory diseases. The attributes of a garnet as a birthstone are that it is believed to endow the wearer with friendship, power and constancy when born under the sign of Aquarius. Though found in other colours, it is the dark red garnet which, by reason of its colour as well as its nature, is the true birthstone for Aquarius.

Next in the Zodiacal sequence is the amethyst, which is the birthstone for those born from 19th February to 20th March. These gems, too, have a long history—in fact there is a necklace extant, found in Greece, which had belonged to a Mycenaean princess of 3,000 years ago. It has always been known as the stone of authority and has been much used for papal and bishops' rings. The word 'amethyst' comes from the Greek for immunity from intoxication and wearing the stone was supposed to give the wearer freedom from drunkenness. The ancients also believed that it changed colour to warn the wearer of impending ill-health. It was said to be the favourite stone of St Valentine, whose birthday fell in this period, and he was said to have worn a ring set with an amethyst which was appropriately engraved with a representation of Cupid—so legend goes. For those whose birthstone it is, the amethyst is a symbol of serenity and is said to have the ability to inspire virtue and high ideals.

For those born in the next period—between 21st March and 20th April, under Aries—the birthstone is the lovely aquamarine. This is supposed to be the symbol of happiness and of everlasting youth, and of courage. It has the changing shades of the sea, varying from pale, delicate blue to clear pastel green. In a poem written in the fourteenth century, *The Vision of Piers the Plowman*, the wearer of an aquamarine was said to be miraculously protected from the ravages of poisoning. At one time it was believed that the stone quickened the intellect, but according to Camillus Leonardus its essential quality was to cure distemper of the throat and jaws. There is a secondary birthstone for this period—the bloodstone, a dark green chalcedony spotted with red, again with a medical legend because in the Middle Ages it was actually often used for the treatment of blood poisoning and the healing of wounds. It is not a pretty stone, however, and is seldom, if ever, used for feminine jewellery.

Those born in the period from 21st April to 20th May and come under the sign of Taurus have as their birthstone the loveliest of them all—the diamond, whose influence over human affairs is perhaps more powerful than any other gem. It is believed to symbolize innocence and its name comes from the Greek word 'Adamas', meaning indomitable. It was more valued in ancient times for its physical and mystical properties than for its intrinsic worth. It had the legendary power of protecting the wearer from evil, especially when worn on the left side of the person. This belief may well be the subconscious reason for the almost universal choice of diamonds for an engagement ring. In India, tiny diamonds are sprinkled over a baby's head at its naming ceremony to endow the child with the attributes of purity and virtue. The first Queen Elizabeth wore a diamond as a guard against infection, while Napoleon wore one set in the hilt of his sword as a talisman. According to ancient lore, if a diamond was to bring luck it had to be given freely, never coveted and never taken by fraud or force.

Those born under Gemini, from 21st May to 20th June, are almost as fortunate as the Taurians for their birthstone is the beautiful green emerald, as prized today as it was 3,000 years ago when the Egyptians considered it to be a stone of the gods. In those days sacred images and idols had flashing emerald eyes, and the Mohammedans believed that a rough emerald inscribed with a verse of the Koran was a talisman of immortality. They also regarded the emerald as a symbol of constancy and of true affection—a belief which still persists. It has always been associated with eyesight and was perhaps the origin of the belief that green is the most restful colour. A polished emerald was once believed to have the power of restoring failing eyesight when held against the closed lids, and Nero is recorded as having used an emerald to lengthen his vision when watching gladiators in the arena. But the emerald is perhaps best known as the talisman of sailors. Suspended from the neck and worn against the skin, an uncut emerald is supposed to protect fishermen and sailors from perils of drowning. Its qualities as a birthstone are love and success, so that it is appropriate that it should have been described as the favourite stone of Venus, goddess of Love.

Between 21st June and 21st July the Zodiacal sign is Cancer and those born in this period have the choice of three birthstones—the pearl, the moonstone and the alexandrite, in that order. The primary birthstone, the pearl, is the only gem which attains perfection in the sea. It is said to confer upon the Cancerian the great gift of vitality and it is, too, the symbol of health, energy, beauty and thought. It was the favourite gem of Diana, protectress of young girls, and is traditionally the most appropriate gem for the *jeune fille*. The moonstone, the secondary birthstone for this period, is a milky-white stone with faint bluish lights, and was once regarded as a love charm during the waxing of the moon, while in the moon's waning the wearer was enabled to foretell the future. The alexandrite has the natural power of taking on a rich green colour by daylight and a deep raspberry-red at night or by artificial light. This again is not a particularly attractive stone and is not used for feminine jewels, though it is occasionally used for men's signet rings.

The blood-red ruby is the birthstone of those born under Leo, from 22nd July to 21st August. This gem, like the sapphire, is of the corundum family and is one that has attracted since the beginning of time. Both rubies and sapphires are sometimes found with a natural star-shaped centre and the fascinating thing about these starred gems is that no matter how the gem is cut, each separate piece will have its own six-ray star. For centuries rubies have been credited with the power of attracting love and devotion, and they are supposed also to endow the wearer with contentment. Here again is a stone which was credited in the Middle Ages with having particular medicinal powers, among them the capacity to bring relief in pain, to protect the wearer from drowning and to cure rheumatism. Leo subjects have a secondary birthstone, the cornelian, which was said to ensure the soul's journey from the underworld if it was placed on the neck on the day of burial —that such a belief existed has been substantiated by the finding of cornelians in excavated coffins. The Hebrews and Arabs considered the cornelian to be a charm against plague, while Mabodus attributed to it the quality of stilling angry passions and bringing concord. The Spaniards, on the other hand, claimed that it gave the wearer courage.

For people born under Virgo—from 22nd August to 21st September—married happiness is said to be ensured for those who wear their birthstone, the peridot, a gemstone which owes its peculiarly attractive shade of green to the presence of impurities; when pure it is quite colourless. It was believed that the peridot had the power to overcome mental and physical timidity—the inferiority complex of today. It is the symbol of a happy marriage and is said to bring gladness, serenity and faithfulness to those for whom it is the birthstone. It is also said to symbolize eloquence and persuasiveness. The Crusaders greatly treasured these gemstones.

The beautiful blue sapphire, symbol of clear thinking, is the birthstone of those born between 22nd September and 22nd October under Libra. It is the talisman of St Andrew and was sacred to the god Apollo. Its symbols are peace and virtue and it is said to be a guard against poisons and to give the wearer wisdom. The star-sapphire is particularly lucky for the Librian, giving charm to the wearer and the ability to inspire everlasting love. Its influence is exerted on the first wearer even after it has left her keeping. Though the gem is found in many other colours, it is the true cornflower blue which is the birthstone for this period.

Those born between 23rd October and 21st November come under Scorpio and their birthstone is the opal. Far from being unlucky, as some people believe, it was thought in olden times to be a very lucky gem. It symbolizes hope, faith and good fortune, and is believed to bring romance and lasting love. There *are* superstitions attached to it, for it was worn by blonde women in the belief that it preserved the colour of their hair. Opals are found only where there has been an inland sea, and they are said to combine the fire of the ruby, the sunset purple of the amethyst and the mysterious green depth of the emerald. No two opals are ever alike; no two ever have exactly the same colour variations which makes them highly individual as well as beautiful gems.

Saggitarius is the Zodiacal sign for those born from 22nd November to 20th December, and their birthstone is the topaz, which was believed to have the ability to ward off insomnia and asthma, powers which increased as the moon waxed and decreased as it waned. In addition, it was said that if a topaz was applied to the inside or outside of the nostrils it would stop nose-bleeding. The symbols of the topaz, which ranges in colour from pale yellow to deep sherry brown, are fidelity and true friendship. Besides the golden tones with which the topaz is associated, it does in fact occur in almost all colours, as well as in white.

The last of the Zodiacal signs—Capricorn—rules those born from 21st December to 19th January. The birthstone for this period is the turquoise, a charming blue stone which was known to the ancients as the Turkis or Turkey stone because it was brought from Persia into Europe via Turkey, being finally given its present name by the French. The Turks and the Tibetans especially prized the stone which they regarded as a talisman for horsemen. Tibetans decorated their horses' trappings with turquoise and silver and even in modern times, in some remote parts of Tibet, it was used in place of money in trading transactions. The primary quality of the turquoise as a birthstone is that of bestowing prosperity on the wearer, and symbolizing good fortune and success for Capricornians. Sometimes one sees a turquoise which is greenish in colour, which may indicate that it is a poorish-quality stone, for the best ones are a clear, pale blue. Turquoise matrix, much used in Victorian times for jewellery, is the rock in which the true turquoise is found. Capricornians have a secondary birthstone, the zircon in its blue shade (it is found in many other colours), and this gem is supposed to cheer the heart and give charm to the wearer.

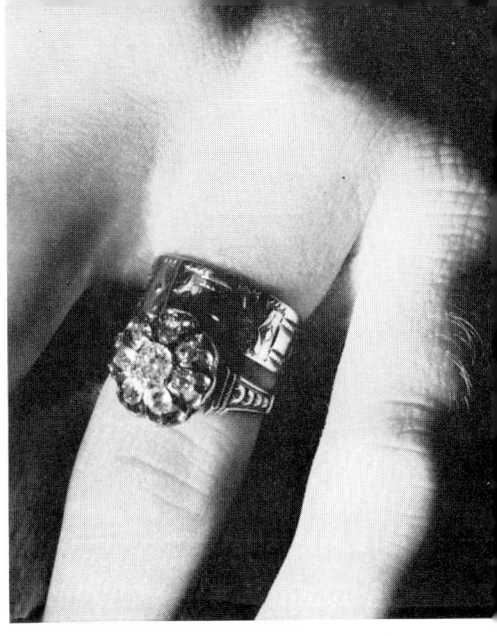

LEFT: Cluster of diamonds favoured a century ago. An engagement ring of gold with a cluster of diamonds. RIGHT: Engagement and wedding ring set of c. 1850. The wedding ring is extremely wide, the fashion of the times.

LEFT: Diamond and fresh-water pearl ring designed by Marvin Hime of Beverly Hills. RIGHT: Modern diamond engagement ring in platinum with a contrasting yellow-gold wedding band achieves a one-ring look; by Lindemann & Company of San Francisco.

A diamond suite by Garrard, consisting of a necklace with matching ear-rings, brooch, and bracelet. Also shown are three rings, an emerald-cut, a marquise-cut, and a brilliant-cut.

An emerald and diamond suite by Garrard. This is a particularly fine example of the combination of artist and craftsman. The search for matching stones for this suite took over six months.

LEFT: Diamond and gold zinnia brooch by Erwin Pearl of New York. RIGHT: A school of diamond fish set in platinum by Bick and Ostor of Montreal.

LEFT: Faraone of Milan gives his impression of a film star in this brooch design with a marquise diamond head. RIGHT: Diamond sailboats with platinum masts, created by Patek Philippe of Geneva.

CHAPTER THIRTEEN

Setting and cutting gems

NOTHING so clearly determines the period of a jewel as the method of its setting. Even the precious metal used is itself a guide, for platinum, one of today's most popular metals for setting gems, was not so used until the second and third decades of the present century, so that a platinum-set jewel can usually be dated by the presence of that metal alone.

Antique jewellery was almost always set in gold, the very earliest examples of centuries ago using pure gold. Silver, too, was used and even appears in some jewels in the British Royal Regalia. Coloured golds, which had a considerable vogue in the mid-twentieth century, are not a new discovery, for green, pink and other coloured golds were achieved as long ago as Tudor times when the use of different alloys transmuted yellow gold into different colours.

In the beginning of jewellery-making in Britain, if one starts in Anglo-Saxon times, the practice was to set gems or slabs of coloured glass into deep, box-like containers in which the gems were flush with the metal. Practically all the museum pieces extant for this period show this form of setting in which stones were used to give colour and pattern rather than to display their own intrinsic beauty. Since gem cutting was almost unknown there the gems in consequence had form and colour but no 'life' and the settings were simply functional containers for them. This flush-setting, incidentally, persists today in at least one form of jewellery—in men's signet rings in which a tablet gem is sometimes sunk into a solid bed of metal.

Modern craftsmanship in setting precious jewellery has made immense strides in recent years and the developments in this field have been particularly noteworthy. Primarily the aim has been—and is—to achieve a strong yet almost invisible setting so that the stone is fully displayed instead of being, iceberg-like, three parts submerged by a setting designed more for safety than for aesthetic beauty. This 'invisible' quality has been gained chiefly by the use of piercing and hand-sawing, developing logically from the open, lace-like fretting used in the earlier attempts at lightness. The aim of the designers of rings, for example, is to show precious stones as prominently as possible by raising them from their background and having the minimum of metal showing in actual contact with the gems. This invisible setting does in fact have the effect of making a comparatively small gem look much larger and more important while the use of a lightly pierced framework allows a greater refraction of light through the gem, thus enhancing its beauty.

This treatment is naturally most successful with diamonds, though similar settings are just as effectively used for brooches, clips and necklaces in which the diamonds, rubies, emeralds and sapphires seem to be held by suction only. Despite their 'invisibility' such settings are just as secure as the older, more solid-looking ones. Sometimes, when a rather small diamond is used for instance, an additional coronel, like a metal washer, is added to the top of the gem setting, raising it up to make the stone look higher and therefore bigger. Such a setting is known as an 'illusion' setting, which is exactly what it is: it gives the gem the illusion of being a larger stone than it actually is.

Much attention is being paid today, too, to the 'movement' of jewellery, and diamond and other jewelled pieces are often mounted on a fine, closely whorled spiral spring, which as well as giving a three-dimensional effect also keeps the jewel in constant movement so that the piece quivers and sends out scintillating rays from the faceted gems with the wearer's merest movement. This is a revival of a Victorian technique seen, for example, in a modern diamond bird brooch mounted on a spring at its centre back which projects the bird about an eighth of an inch from the pin. Though small—two inches from tip to tip—the jewel quivers and gleams arrestingly so that it appears to be much more impressive than its size warrants. This is the sort of jewel to appeal, as it undoubtedly does, to the woman who likes smaller jewels, but likes them to be dramatic in their own way.

Settings which tax the ingenuity and skill of the craftsman are those designed for modern convertible jewels. To make a necklace or a tiara that breaks up into several complete jewels so that each fulfils its function as a separate entity, yet join together to make a perfectly co-ordinated whole, calls upon all the constructional, fine-precision skill of which the craftsman is capable.

Another notable advance in settings has been the achievement of a textile-like suppleness. Loops and bows of rubies and diamonds, set in platinum, give expression to this trend in a modern necklace which lies on the contours of the neck with the suppleness of a fabric. Another example is seen in a five-row bracelet of pavé-set baguette sapphires with a central row of similarly cut and set emeralds which is just as flexible as a piece of ribbon velvet—and invisibly set in platinum so that the colours are quite solid. To achieve this hidden setting a groove is cut in each gem below the top and it is then slid into fine platinum 'channels' like trolley tracks which run through this groove and hold the stones immovably.

'Articulated' jewellery is another outstanding modern technique, seen in a butterfly brooch which can be worn with wings outstretched or partly closed, and in a rose, completely diamond-set, which can be worn as a rosebud with folded petals or as a full-blown rose with fully opened petals. These are further developments of setting techniques which call for the highest degree of fine precision work and engineering skill.

Medieval styles of setting used a simple turned over edge of metal to contain the stones. This setting is still used today for the less expensive gems such as amethysts, turquoises and so on. In calibre settings a design is achieved by gems cut to special sizes to make a graduated effect such as, say, a brooch in the form of a fan, for which the gems will be cut to a special measure—calibre—to taper in size from the width at the top of the open fan to the narrow point of the handle, each stone fitting into its appointed place to arrive at the design envisaged. Pavé-set stones are also used to give form to a three-dimensional jewel. Set this way there is no sign, from the top of the jewel, of the precious metal used to hold the stones. Pavé is the term used to describe an area of evenly set and closely matched stones.

Box setting, dating from thousands of years ago, is sometimes used today, comprising sections of metal into which the stone is laid—simple but effective. Such box settings are called collet when, as is often done, the 'box' is filed down to make triangular openings in its sides. This allows light to reach the part of the stone held in the setting and is an improvement on the wholly solid metal box setting, especially for diamonds. Fine claws or coronet settings are mostly used in rings—coronet when the stone is round; claw setting when it is rectangular. For small stones set either in a cluster of equal sizes or with a central large stone surrounded by smaller ones the millegrain setting is generally used. In this the recess in which the stone is set has its upper metal edge broken up into a line of tiny beads or 'millegrains', reflecting minute points of light so that they look like diamond points. Settings designed to hold clusters of stones generally have a cage-like back with a central group of eight claws to hold a large central stone.

In the techniques of ring settings there have been many interesting developments in the past few decades. Modern ring shoulders are almost architecturally designed, flowing from the shank up to the gems to give a sculptured look to the whole, the setting leading up logically to the gem or 'table' of the ring.

In the field of gem cutting the lapidary's art finds endless expression, for on the shape to which he cuts the gem will depend the full extraction of its inherent beauty. Beginning with the primitive method of simply polishing the gem, or *cabochon*-cut (the oldest form of all), the craft has developed through the centuries to faceting—the rose-cut of the Middle Ages—to the emerald, or step-cut, brilliant-cut, baguette, baton, marquise, pendeloque, lozenge, navette or boat shape, drop or pear shape, briollet, bead and other cuts used today. Most of these forms of cutting are used in the case of diamonds and other gems having a refraction of light; they are seldom used with opaque gems. In the case of the former gems they are employed as the shape of the gem and the possible loss of size determine. A combination of brilliant-cut crown with step-cut back is quite often used for some gems and is known as 'mixed-cut'.

Like the silversmith, the lapidary clings to the simple tools of past centuries, though many up-to-date machines have been evolved to supersede the hand-held gem-peg of primitive times with which many lapidaries still prefer to work. The craft is a highly skilled, very important one.

With transparent stones the lapidary's object is to produce a clean stone that will allow light to pass into it and be reflected by means of polished facets on the back of the stone, the light passing through the front. Opaque stones, however, such as opals, moonstones, turquoises and so on, are not faceted and are cut and polished to a *cabochon* dome surface as there is no natural light to be reflected through the stone. Both types of cutting of precious stones are much simpler for the lapidary than is diamond cutting for which, owing to the extreme hardness of the gem, great pressure is necessary. Expert lapidaries have to have, almost above all else, an unfailing sense of touch.

Briefly, the first step is for the craftsman cutter to fix the gem firmly by means of cement on to a kind of wooden penholder —the 'peg'. The other end of the holder is held securely against a rest, or 'jamb peg'. This gadget is fixed to his working bench at the right-hand side of a revolving metal lap with which the surface of the stone is brought into contact. This lap is charged with diamond powder, emery or carborundum (according to the nature of the gem to be cut, e.g. only diamond will cut a diamond). Measuring about an inch in thickness and about twelve inches in diameter, the metal lap revolves horizontally, either by hand or by power.

At the first operation the rough shape has been fashioned, governed to some extent by the necessity for removing any imperfections which may be present in the gem. When all the facets have been cut—varying in number according to the type of cut—rose, brilliant, and so on—the gem still presents a dull surface. This is where the polisher comes into the operation, using the identical equipment to that of the cutter except that in place of the cutting material on the metal lap there is a fine polishing material such as rottenstone. As the lap revolves he presses each rough face in turn against the polishing material on the revolving lap to give it a brilliant polish. Great delicacy of touch and pressure are essential at this stage because the polisher has to be sure that the pressure, whilst strong enough to produce a high polish on each facet, is yet not strong enough to enlarge its size—achieved with such meticulous accuracy by the cutter.

For round stones the brilliant cut is used. This has no fewer than 58 facets—33 on the front, or crown, of the stone, and 25 facets on the back, or pavilion. There is the large octagonal table facet surrounded by 32 smaller facets, described by the expert as 'four bezels, four lozenges, eight stars, eight skew and eight skill facets'. The back (the part which is held by the setting) is pyramid shaped and has a small culet facet at the very apex with 24 other facets—four pavilions, four quoins, eight cross and eight skill facets.

One of the most difficult tasks with which the lapidary has to contend is the recutting of gems which have been cut by native workmen in the East whose crude methods often produce a misshapen form and haphazardly placed facets. It takes great skill and patience to recut such gems so as to show their hitherto concealed or blurred inherent beauty. Often the work results inevitably in loss of size, but this is more than redeemed by the greatly enhanced brilliance which is revealed by expert cutting.

CHAPTER FOURTEEN

Some famous gems and their history

MOUNTAIN OF LIGHT, Star of the East, Eureka: names of poetical cadence which might describe planets, mountains or—racehorses. To the cognoscenti, however, they instantly conjure up visions of diamonds; gems of fascinating history, fabulous worth, and unparalleled beauty. The story of each could make a chapter in itself, an enthralling tale of adventure, daring and, all too often, disaster and death. Many of the world-famous diamonds have disappeared unaccountably; many hide their lustre in safe deposits; many, fortunately, have survived to grace the British Crown Jewels and the museums and art centres of the world where the eye may feast on the brilliant beauty of the gems while the imagination is stimulated by the legends with which they are clothed by their chequered history.

It is a temptation to wander slowly through each step of the way traversed by famous gems; necessity demands that only a brief outline may be given to some of the better-known named gems (alphabetically and not by size and importance) within the compass of this book.

The **Akbar Shah** is a fine diamond which weighed 116 carats when rough; 75 carats when cut, and 71 carats when it was recut. According to legend this gem was, like the Koh-i-Noor, one of the eyes of the Peacock Throne of the Great Moguls and was named after Shah Akbar. He was the grandfather of the Shah Jehan whose Taj Mahal is one of the Seven Wonders of the World. The names of both Shah Akbar and of Shah Jehan were inscribed in Arabic characters on the diamond, a felicitous gesture which served to identify the diamond when, after its disappearance during the first half of the eighteenth century, it reappeared in Constantinople (Istambul) in 1866 under the name of the Shepherd Stone. It was eventually purchased by an English merchant who brought it to London. There it was recut to a stone weighing 71 carats and sold to the Gaekwar of Baroda, in whose possession it presumably remained, for about £35,000. In the recutting of the diamond the inscribed names of the two great rulers were eliminated, but they had served their purpose of identifying the stone for all time.

The **Darya-i-Noor,** weighing 186 carats in the rough, is a rose-cut diamond whose romantic name means 'Sea of Light'. It was carried off by the Perso-Tartar conqueror, Nadir Shah, when he plundered the Delhi Treasury in 1739. With the **Taj-e-Mah** diamond of 146 carats weight, the Darya-i-Noor was set in a pair of bracelets and in this setting remained in the possession of the Persian kings for centuries. In 1955 the Darya-i-Noor was offered for sale in Pakistan, and again in 1959, when it was then in the possession of the Nawab of Dacca.

Dresden Green. This is a wonderful almond-shaped apple-green diamond of purest water, its colour making it one of the rarest gems in the world, though it is only 41 carats in weight. It was bought by Augustus the Strong, the Elector of Saxony and King of Poland, who died in 1733, and remained in royal possession during which time it was displayed, coincidentally, in the famous Green Vaults under the Dresden Palace. The Palace was bombed and severely damaged during the Second World War, but the Dresden Green diamond, together with other important jewels, was hidden in a fortress and so survived the bombardment. In 1945 the Saxon Crown Jewels were confiscated by the Soviet Trophies Organization and taken to Russia. In 1959 there were reports that the treasures had been restored to Dresden, but there was no mention of the Dresden Green diamond among them and it is believed to have been retained for the Moscow Kremlin.

The **English Dresden** diamond which weighed $119\frac{1}{2}$ carats in the rough, and $76\frac{1}{2}$ carats when it was cut, is a comparatively new stone, for it was not discovered until 1857 in the Bagagem Mine in Brazil, the third largest diamond to come from that mine.

It is not green and it has no connexion with the city of Dresden; its name comes from that of Mr E. Dresden, the London merchant who bought it in the rough. Mr Dresden had the diamond cut in Amsterdam in a drop form weighing 76½ carats, and sold it to an East India merchant for a reported £40,000. That owner fell upon bad times and circumstances compelled him to sell it. The buyer was the Gaekwar of Baroda, but the diamond is now believed to be owned by Cursejjee Fardoonji of India.

The **Eugénie** is a beautiful, perfectly cut brilliant oval diamond of 51 carats which first belonged to the Empress Catherine II of Russia, who in turn gave it to Potemkin, one of her favourites, in recognition of his military services to Russia. Later on the Emperor Napoleon III of France purchased the diamond from Potemkin's great-niece, to whom it had presumably been given or was inherited by her, for bestowal as a bridal gift on the Empress Eugénie, after whom the diamond is named. After Napoleon's downfall the stone came into the market and was sold to that ardent collector of famous diamonds, the Gaekwar of Baroda, for £15,000. Like other of the Gaekwar's prized possessions, the diamond was sold later and is now said to be owned by a woman—Mrs N. J. Dady of Bombay—which leads one to speculate that this diamond with a feminine name is destined always to be owned by a woman.

The **Eureka** diamond is most aptly named, for in 1866 some Boer children playing by the banks of the Orange River in South Africa found a large pebble, nearly white in colour and looking like a lump of alum or washing soda. They showed it to Van Niekerk, a neighbour, who took it to several traders who refused to believe it had any value. Finally he sent it to a government agent who recognized it as a diamond of 21 carats, which Sir Philip Wodehouse, Governor of the Cape, bought for £500 and later exhibited at the 1889 Paris Exhibition. In more recent times it formed part of a diamond bangle on which was engraved 'The Eureka Diamond. First found in South Africa.' It lay in a blue velvet-lined case inscribed in gold lettering: 'The centre stone of this bracelet was the "Eureka" diamond, being first discovered in South Africa. The remaining stones are all South African, mostly from the mines of Kimberley.' This was sold at Christie's in 1946, and the famous Eureka diamond from the bangle is now set in a ring owned by Mr Peter Locan, the final cutting having reduced it to 10¾ carats, and was one of the many exquisite exhibits at 'The Ageless Diamond' Exhibition held at Christie's in 1959.

The **Excelsior** diamond, weighing 995 carats in the rough, was, until the finding of the Cullinan twelve years later, the largest known diamond in the world. It was discovered in the Jagersfontein mine in South Africa in 1893 and is irregular in shape, with a cleavage face on one side, of excellent blue-white colour and quality. It was not cut until 1903, when the famous firm of Asschers in Amsterdam cut it to yield 21 stones adding up to a total of 373¾ carats—a loss in weight of 62·4 per cent. The largest stone cut from the Excelsior was a 70-carat marquise of exquisite beauty. Another marquise of 18 carats cut from the Excelsior was exhibited by the De Beers Company at the New York World Fair in 1939.

The **Florentine** diamond is one of the coloured diamonds—a clear citron yellow of great fascination and beauty, with its origin shrouded in mystery. Legend has it that the diamond was worn in his cap by Charles the Bold, Duke of Burgundy. In 1476 the Duke suffered a great defeat, losing a tremendous amount of arms and booty, including this diamond which was picked up on the battlefield by a soldier who, thinking it was a chunk of glass, sold it to a local priest for two shillings. The wonderful yellow diamond changed hands many times, one of its owners being Pope Julius II. There are those who claim that the authentic history of the diamond dates only from 1657, when Tavernier, visiting Florence on his pretty well interminable travels, examined a diamond of a citron-yellow colour among the treasures of the reigning Duke of Tuscany. That diamond eventually passed into the possession of the Austrian Royal House through the marriage between Maria Theresa and Francis Stephen of Lorraine, late Grand Duke of Tuscany. The bride was said to have worn the diamond as a brooch. It remained in the Crown Jewels of Vienna for several generations and was valued at no less than $450,000 cut as a double rose of 126 facets on an irregular nine-sided outline. After the tragic collapse of the Austrian Empire the Crown Jewels, including the brooch with the 'Florentine' diamond went into exile with the Royal Family. Its history since then is uncertain, but when the Germans invaded Austria they carried off a yellow diamond which was restored to the city by the American authorities at the end of the Second World War. It is, of course, possible that this yellow diamond is not the Florentine but another one which was known as the Austrian Yellow Brilliant, once set in the Hapsburg Crown.

The **Great Mogul** diamond is a product of the fabulous Golconda mines—the Kollur, near Golconda—and weighed 787 carats in the rough; 280 carats when it was cut. Discovered in the mid-seventeenth century, it was among the treasures of Shah Jehan, the owner of the Darya-i-Noor, who completed the magnificent Peacock Throne. In 1665 Shah Jehan's son Aurangzeb showed it to Tavernier who described it later as being in shape like 'half an egg cut through the middle'. The diamond was believed subsequently to have been among the loot carried off by the Persians under the command of Nadir Shah after the sack of Delhi. Some argue that the Great Mogul is in fact the Darya-i-Noor; others that it is the diamond that Prince Orloff gave Catherine the Great of Russia—the diamond that bears his name, the Orloff—and that it is possible that the Great Mogul does not exist as such. It is quite probable that the diamond was cut into two or more stones to escape identification—a fate which has been known to befall other famous diamonds.

The **Hope** diamond is perhaps the best known of all diamonds because so very much has been written about it and the legends that surround it. It has been described as the gem with a curse, and certainly some harrowing stories have been written about the fate that has invariably followed its ownership—violent death (including being torn to death by wild dogs!), suicide, financial disaster and so on. Factually, it is a wonderful diamond of deep blue colour which weighed $112\frac{1}{4}$ carats in the rough and only $44\frac{1}{2}$ carats when it was cut into its present shape. Its history is linked with the **Blue Tavernier** and it is likely that both names refer to the same gem, the name Hope having been given to the diamond comparatively recently after the man who bought it in the mid-nineteenth century—Henry Thomas Hope, a banker and keen collector of gems. The Blue Tavernier was found in the Kollur diamond mines near Golconda, and was secured by the French expert Tavernier in 1642. Together with other jewels, Tavernier sold the diamond to Louis XIV in 1668, when it weighed 67 carats after cutting and polishing, and it became a showpiece of the French Regalia. During the French Revolution it was stolen from the Garde Meuble with other French treasures and from that point in history all trace of it was lost. In 1830 a diamond of similarly rare deep blue colour came on to the London market, and was bought by Mr Hope for £18,000, though it is possible, if this is the Blue Tavernier, that it had been smuggled out of France during the Revolution and recut to escape detection. In 1908 Abdul Hamid, Sultan of Turkey, acquired it for a reputed price of £80,000, and three years later it appeared offered for sale at Cartier's in Paris, from whom it was bought by the late Mrs Edward B. McLean of Washington, a famous society hostess renowned for her wonderful jewellery in which she presented a dazzling appearance at the Opera House and other functions. At the sale of her jewel collection in 1949, attended by experts and connoisseurs from all over the world, it was bought by Mr Harry Winston, the equally famous diamond merchant of New York. He, with great generosity and public-spiritedness, put an end to the legend of bad luck and at the same time gave the public an opportunity of seeing the gem at close quarters by presenting it to the Smithsonian Institute in Washington. The magnitude of the gesture can be appreciated when one learns that the famous diamond was then valued at one million dollars.

The **Jonker** diamond, a truly magnificent gem weighing 726 carats in the rough, was picked up by a digger named Jacobus

Jonker in the alluvial diggings at Elandsfontein, near Pretoria, in 1934. The diamond had a cleavage face, but was otherwise rounded in shape, of a beautiful blue-white colour; indeed some considered it to be the finest gem ever found. It was acquired by the Diamond Trading Corporation for £70,000 and was eventually sold to Mr Harry Winston for a reported $700,000, after which it was cut into twelve perfect gems—eleven emerald-cut, and a marquise-cut, the total carats being 358. The largest gem to be cut from the Jonker diamond is emerald-cut in 58 facets, first of 142·9 carats, then later recut to 125·6 carats. Ex-King Farouk of Egypt bought the stone, which at that time was valued at $1,000,000. Following his deposition and exile in 1952 it was reported to be in the 'custody' of the Egyptian Government. In 1959, however, there were rumours that the Queen of Nepal was to be seen wearing the Jonker diamond.

The **Jubilee** diamond is another large, fine stone, weighing 650 carats in the rough and 245 carats when cut into a faultless cushion-cut gem notable for its clarity, whiteness and brilliance. Discovered in the Jagersfontein mine in 1895, it was first called the 'Reitz' after the President of the Orange Free State and later renamed the Jubilee when it was cut in the year of Queen Victoria's Jubilee in 1897. The diamond was shown, and greatly admired, in the Paris Exhibition of 1900, and was owned for many years by the late Sir Dorab Tata, the Indian industrialist. It was sold again in 1937 through Cartier's to an undisclosed purchaser, but the present owner is Mr Harry Winston who exhibited the diamond in Geneva in 1960, when its value was declared to be $2,000,000.

The **Koh-i-Noor** diamond almost needs no describing, for it must be the best known of all the famous gems. This colossal stone was 800 carats in the rough, 186 Indian carats when cut, and 108·43 English carats when it was recut in Britain. It is said to have been found in Golconda and to have a known history going back to 1304 when it was in the possession of one of the ancient royal families—the Rajahs of Malwa. Two centuries later it was acquired by Sultan Baber, founder of the Mogul

Dynasty and it remained in the possession of successive Emperors. In the early eighteenth century when the warlike and indefatigable Nadir Shan invaded North-West India and plundered Delhi, he obtained possession of the Koh-i-Noor as well as of other large diamonds. When the conqueror first set eyes on the coveted gem he is said to have cried 'Koh-i-Noor!' (Mountain of Light) and so it was named. On his death the conquered Empire fell and after many adventures the diamond returned to India, coming into the hands of Ranjit Singh—the Lion of the Punjab—in 1833. It remained in the Jewel Chamber of Lahore until 1849, in which year the stone was taken by the East India Company as partial indemnity following on the Sikh Wars in the Punjab. In 1850 it was presented to Queen Victoria by Lord Dalhousie at a levée held to mark the 250th anniversary of the founding of the Company. When it was shown at the Great Exhibition of 1851, held in Hyde Park, London, great disappointment was expressed by everyone that the stone did not show more fire. This criticism helped to decide Queen Victoria to have the stone recut in 1862 to a shallow brilliant, the cutting reducing the diamond to a weight of 108 carats. This highly important and responsible task was entrusted to a diamond cutter from Amsterdam named Voorsanger who spent thirty-eight days in London cutting the diamond. Queen Victoria wore it as brooch, and on her death it was transferred to the Regalia and set in the centre of the front cross patée of the State Crown, first of Queen Alexandra and then of Queen Mary. It was finally set in the crown made in 1937 for the coronation of King George VI and Queen Elizabeth.

The **Nassak** diamond, of unknown origin, was cut to a weight of 90 carats, then recut to 80 carats, and again to 43 carats. It was said to have first appeared in the temple of the Hindu god Siva at Nasik (which was formerly called Nassak), a once-famous place of pilgrimage situated about a hundred miles from Bombay. Some time later the diamond was removed from the temple in order to raise money by the local Mahratta rulers for their campaigns against the British. It next appeared in 1818 as part of the Deccan booty which fell into the hands of the East

India Company, who valued it at £30,000. Soon afterwards the Company had it brought to London where, on its being offered for sale, it was bought by the then Crown Jewellers, Rundell, Bridge & Co. It was they who decided that the diamond's facets should be recut to obtain more fire and there ensued the remarkable task of recutting while preserving the triangular shape in 90 facets at a sacrifice of only about ten carats. In 1837 the diamond was bought by the Marquess of Westminster who had it set in the hilt of his dress sword. The Nassak remained in his family for many years, and was exhibited in 1927 at Mauboussin's showrooms in New York. It was brought back to this country but soon afterwards was bought by Mr Harry Winston and returned with him to New York where the new owner had it refashioned into a modern 43-carat emerald-cut stone and in that form sold it to the firm of Trabert & Hoeffer. Finally it was bought by Mrs William B. Leeds of New York who, it is believed, still owns it.

The **Niarchos** diamond weighed $426\frac{1}{2}$ carats in the rough and $128\frac{1}{4}$ carats when cut. It was found in the Premier mine in 1951, and was described by the late Sir Ernest Oppenheimer as having 'the most perfect colour of any diamond he had ever seen'. This diamond, too, was acquired by Mr Harry Winston and was cut into a pear-shaped gem with 143 facets, valued at $2,000,000. With a gem of this size and wonderful quality the cutting was a tremendously responsible task and took a total of 1,400 hours to accomplish. Two other stones, an emerald-cut of 40 carats and a marquise of 28 carats, were also fashioned from the diamond. It is the largest portion of the three which is the Niarchos diamond, so named when it was bought by Mr Stavros S. Niarchos, the Greek shipowner. This latter diamond was the cynosure of all eyes when its matchless purity was displayed among other world-famous diamonds at 'The Ageless Diamond' Exhibition in London in 1959.

The **Nizam,** which weighed 340 carats in the rough, was a Golconda discovery. Of all the mines in the Golconda area the Kollur mine on the Kisna river was the most productive and there is a strong probability that the Nizam was found in that mine. As the diamond fields of Golconda are situated in the Nizam of Hyderabad's territory the stone was named after him. There has been much speculation as to the actual weight of the diamond when it was found, which has been variously estimated as between 277 and 340 carats, though the latter weight is thought to have been more accurate. According to one authority the diamond originally weighed 440 carats and was mysteriously broken in 1857 in the year of the Indian Mutiny. So far as is known the diamond is still uncut and is in the possession of the present Nizam of Hyderabad, reputed to be one of the richest men in the world and to have the most priceless collection of gems.

The **Orloff**, 300 carats in the rough and 199·6 carats when cut, was discovered at the beginning of the seventeenth century, again in the Kollur mine at Golconda. Its early history is obscure, but some authorities say it was at one time in the treasure house of the Shah Jehan. On the other hand there is a legend to the effect that the stone was stolen by a French soldier, one stormy night, from the eye of an idol in a Brahmin temple near Trichinopoly in Madras, and that it was sold by him to the captain of an English ship who, in turn, sold it to a London dealer at the end of his voyage. Whatever its previous movements and adventures, the diamond turned up in Amsterdam in 1774, where it was bought by Prince Gregory Orloff, favourite of Catherine the Great and one of the leaders of the conspiracy which led to the downfall of her husband, Peter III, in 1762. At one time, history has it, the Empress considered marrying Orloff, but the plan was frustrated by his enemies and he fell from favour. He bought the diamond in the hope that it would serve to reinstate him in Catherine's favour but this plan failed, and though the Empress graciously accepted the offering it availed Orloff nothing. Subsequently she had this superb rose-cut diamond of exceptional purity mounted in the Imperial Sceptre and it is now one of the most notable of famous gems in the Diamond Treasury of the U.S.S.R. in Moscow. It has been recorded that Orloff, who was by no means rich, bought the diamond on the instalment plan for a sum of 400,000 roubles, to be repaid over a period of seven years—a galling yoke to have placed about his neck to no avail.

The **Sancy** diamond is not in the 'enormous' category, but it is a very fine stone, weighing 55 carats, with an enthralling history. It was bought in Constantinople in the sixteenth century by Nicholas Harlai, Seigneur de Sancy at the Court of Henry III, son of Catherine de' Medici. Henry IV borrowed it on one occasion to give as security for a loan. A messenger was dispatched with the diamond but on his way was beset by thieves and brutally murdered. De Sancy, convinced that his unfortunate servant's loyalty would never suffer him to surrender the treasure with which he had been entrusted, even to the point of death, set out in search of his body. His faith, and the man's pathetic devotion to duty, were proved to have been well founded, for an examination De Sancy had made of the corpse disclosed that rather than yield the gem to the thieves, he had swallowed it. With due reverence the diamond was removed from the dead man's stomach and his remains decently interred. The diamond is next recorded as being bought by Queen Elizabeth I, in whose inventory it was described as 'one fayre dyamonde, cutt in Fawcetts, Bought of Sancy'. Later it was owned by Charles I and James II who, when he fled to France, sold it to Louis XIV. It was stolen from the Garde Meuble in Paris in 1792 at the same time as the Hope and the Regent diamonds. It is next heard of in 1865, after having passed through many different ownerships. In 1867 it was shown at the Paris Exhibition held that year, where it was seen and bought by the Maharajah of Patiala. The Sancy is now in the possession of the Astor family and was worn by Nancy, Lady Astor, on several occasions, notably at the State Opening of Parliament.

Of the famous coloured gems to be noted is the priceless ruby of the size of a man's hand which the King of Ceylon was said to have owned in the thirteenth century. It is interesting on account of the firm belief held by its owner that it had the power to prolong youth. Certainly there seems to have been some basis for the belief. Every night and morning the King rubbed the stone over his face and neck as a regular ritual and when he died at the age of ninety he was said to have the complexion of a young man, unblemished and unwrinkled. One of the finest emeralds known was said to be one of 136 carats which used to belong to the Tsars of Russia and is now among the Soviet treasures, but an emerald statuette which was found in a tiny shop in a back street of Amritsar in August 1960 has made the Russian emerald seem small by comparison. The statuette, which stands ten inches high, weighs about forty ounces and is valued at $112,500.

The wonderful Colombian emerald and diamond parure of the former Grand Duchess Feodorovna is now in the possession of the Soviet Government. Among carved emeralds one of the most beautiful is that given to Queen Mary when she visited India for the Durbar. This is among the finest examples of emerald carving in existence, a gem which Queen Mary wore as a pendant. Another notable carved gem is the beautiful ruby in the Duke of Marlborough's family jewel collection, which bears an engraving of the mythological dog Sirius. Also in this collection is the Marie Antoinette pearl necklace which was bought by the eighth Duke of Marlborough for his American wife, on whom it was greatly admired.

The famous Hanoverian pearls are another 'jewel' of interesting history. By a decision of the House of Lords these were, during Queen Victoria's reign, 'vested as heirlooms for ever in the British Crown'. The situation of disputed ownership arose on the severance of the Kingdoms of Great Britain and Hanover from what had hitherto been one sovereignty. When this happened, the Duke of Cumberland, uncle of Queen Victoria, claimed the jewels which had come to this country with George I. It was, however, proved that the pearls had, in fact, originally been taken from this country by Princess Elizabeth, eldest daughter of James I, on her marriage to the Elector Palatine of the Rhine. Princess Elizabeth was proved to be a Stuart ancestress from whom Queen Victoria was more directly descended than was the Duke. Armed with this incontrovertible 'proof of ownership' the pearls were accordingly vested in the British Crown, though Queen Victoria seldom wore them. Queen Alexandra, however, formed a liking for the pearls and wore them often. Originally the pearls were believed to have been bought from Mary, Queen of Scots, who sold them—at far below their value, it has been said—to Queen Elizabeth I. Of single pearls, perhaps the finest is the famous round pearl named the 'Paragon' reputed to be owned by the Maharajah of Baroda. This exquisite gem weighs 48 grains and is of incomparable lustre.

CHAPTER FIFTEEN

On choosing jewels

THERE is an art in choosing jewellery, not sufficiently exercised. Jewels are meant to adorn and to express individuality but often are acquired simply as a status symbol. This is unfair to the designer and the creative craftsman, for a jewel is a work of art and should be chosen in relation to the recipient's colouring, age, type and personality; a woman is not a Christmas tree to be hung indiscriminately with sparkling baubles. Ideally a jewel of any importance should be custom-made and considering the cost of a fine piece of jewellery it is surprising that so few are specially designed with the wearer in mind.

Those jewels which have been so designed have a greatly enhanced charm and value for the recipient and where this trouble is taken it is immensely stimulating to the jewellery designer and a welcome challenge to his creative talents—one in which he will co-operate with enthusiasm.

Even if one does not go to these lengths, much more could be done in the choice of jewels in relation to the woman who will wear them; far too often jewels are chosen simply on their value and appearance without particular thought about their appropriateness.

A famous portrait painter has expressed the view that only two gems are universally becoming to every type, age and personality—pearls and diamonds. These, he contends, can be worn at all times through life by all women. This may be basically true but even so, given the acceptance that these gems are universally becoming, the way in which they are used and set can make them less appealing and effective than they might otherwise be. For example, no woman with a short, full neck will be suited by a dog collar of diamonds or close-to-the-throat triple necklace of pearls. Though the gems themselves are becoming, the style in which they are made up can completely spoil their effect.

This same painter expresses a preference for pearls as 'conforming to the sculpture of the neck and shoulders'. Granted this, the sculpture of the neck should determine the length and style of the necklace and the size of the pearls. Only the most slender, swan-like neck can successfully be adorned by marble-sized pearls worn close to the base of the throat, while a short neck can be given apparent length and grace by a longer necklace of pearls graduating in size so that the line is tapered away towards the clasp. Since precious jewellery is costly by any standards it is essential it should flatter the wearer; vagaries of fashion, followed simply because they are 'new', should be confined to costume jewellery which can be discarded when the fashion fades, but precious jewellery which will be the heirloom of tomorrow should be selected with more thought to the wearer's own individuality and to successive generations than to passing fashion.

In general jewellery should be proportionate. A petite woman obviously is not suited by a lot of heavy jewellery which will not only tend to dwarf her but will look ostentatious. For such a type lighter, more delicate jewels are best. Tiaras, if worn, should be of openwork design, small, and preferably coming to a point in the centre front. The 'frontlets' of a byegone day are admirably styled for wearing by a small woman and help to give dignity and the appearance of height without being overwhelming. A necklace should carry out the theme of lightness and aim at a pointed rather than a rounded effect. Ear-rings should be of the drop variety (but not of exaggerated length) rather than stud, and bracelets should in general be narrow rather than wide, though several narrow bracelets can be worn together to good effect. Dress clips or brooches should be worn high on the lapel or the shoulder to carry the movement upwards.

The taller woman can wear more jewellery and larger pieces, though it still needs to be selected with care. She is suited by the more imposing type of tiara and the three-dimensional or bib-style necklace. Wide bracelets are becoming to her provided she is slender as well as tall, in fact a broad bracelet is flattering to a slender arm and serves to break the long line from shoulder to wrist. Women with this type of figure can also successfully wear important corsage brooches and clips placed well below the shoulder line, and either imposing chandelier ear-rings, wide as well as long, or massed cluster ear-rings.

Colouring should also receive consideration in choosing individual jewels. Emeralds are attractive when worn by brunettes or blondes and are especially becoming when worn by auburn-haired women. Diamonds suit all colourings, so do pearls though the deep creamy-coloured pearls are less suited to women with rather sallow complexions. Rubies are seen at their best when worn by dark or grey-haired women, while sapphires and aquamarines are especially becoming to blue-eyed, fair-haired and auburn-haired women. Rubies and mixed gemstones in jewels of bizarre design are perfect for the dark-haired, exotic type.

No woman in these days of advanced chemistry of hair-tinting need be classed as 'mousy' haired, but for those who eschew the hairdresser's art and remain this neutral colour, jewels of rich tones will give definition and character, particularly the gems in emerald green and ruby red. For a more subtle effect the pastel tones of aquamarines, amethysts, rose-quartz and zircon can be used to accent the preferred muted note.

In the choice of rings, the size and shape of the hands are important factors. Long, slender fingers present no problem; they are suited to almost any type of ring though they can best wear those of exaggerated size and the large square or circular solitaire. It is the short hand with rather spatulate fingers which calls for more careful selection. Since this latter type is far more usual, jewellers can offer a wide range of designs calculated to flatter it. Marquise-shaped stones are ideal for giving an illusion of length and slenderness to short fingers; next best is the narrow, rectangular-cut stone, with a crossed cluster or two of single stones one above the other as alternatives. A *cabochon*-cut oval stone also helps to 'slenderize' a short finger. The best ring design is one which carries the eye along the finger rather than across it and for this reason a narrow shank is more flattering than a broad one. If a cluster ring is chosen—i.e. a ring with a central stone surrounded by smaller diamonds—it is best to choose one with the surrounding diamonds navette-cut rather than rose- or brilliant-cut. Diamonds, aquamarines and the paler-coloured stones look better than do the darker-hued rubies and sapphires unless these are cut as rectangular solitaires. Where either of these gems is preferred, it will be found that a rectangular central stone flanked simply by a single baguette diamond at either side is more effective and prettier than a circular central stone surrounded by smaller, round stones. In wedding rings a gemmed eternity ring or one in octagonal shape is best, as long as the ring is a narrow one. A broad wedding ring dwarfs the length of the finger and is more suitable for a long-fingered hand with a good space between the knuckles.

Similarly with bracelets; a narrow style is a happier choice for a well-rounded wrist, while a too-thin wrist can effectively wear a broad, chunky bracelet and is especially suited by the popular charm bracelet with its accompanying heavy gold charms of infinite variety.

CHAPTER SIXTEEN

Caring for your jewels

HAVING acquired jewels there is a responsibility on their owners to care for them and to cherish them as they deserve. Many women, owning and undoubtedly loving precious jewels, think they have nothing more to do for them than to wear them with pride and pleasure. While antique furniture, pictures and other *objets d'art* are maintained scrupulously, equally precious jewellery is often considered not to need any maintenance.

Nothing could be more wrong, particularly where pearls are concerned for instance, for they have a 'life' which requires sustenance. It isn't enough to wear jewels and to keep them, when not being worn, in the jewel case. They need care and attention and—above all—they need cleaning and periodical overhaul. Even the otherwise most fastidious women will wear rings that are caked with a layer of soap scum into which minute particles of dust and other foreign matter have settled, gradually forming a film which will dull the gleam of diamonds and of their setting.

Two things are essential—jewels should be kept clean and should be regularly examined by a jeweller to check up on settings, clasps, threading and so on; and they should be properly housed. It is not too often, if jewels are in constant use, to have them checked over every six months by a jeweller. In between those inspections the jewels should be kept in their own individual containers. Obviously diamond pieces need to be kept apart from other jewels and from each other. Diamonds, being the hardest known substance, will easily scratch the surface of other gems as well as their own surface. Most jewels are bought in their own cases, and where space allows they should always be replaced in these cases after being worn, for they are specially designed to hold the jewels. Small jewels, like rings, brooches and ear-rings, can, however, if space does not allow of their being kept in their boxes, be housed in little individual chamois leather bags so that they do not come into contact with each other in a communal jewel case. Pearls should never be mixed with other, gem-set jewellery as their surface is easily scratched and damaged.

The beauty of diamonds and other precious gems depends on the freedom of light refraction through the stone. This can be quite perceptibly dimmed if the underside of the gem is not scrupulously clean. If dirt has been allowed to accumulate to any degree it becomes a matter for the jeweller to give the jewels the special treatment which will remove the dirt without harming the gem or its setting. But the day-to-day care of jewels, in between the regular expert attention recommended, can be done at home. Soapsuds, which form a film in which foreign matter collects imperceptibly, can be removed by careful brushing with a small hog's bristle brush dipped in rubbing alcohol. With this the backs of the gems and the interstices of the setting should be carefully cleaned, following this removal of the accretion by washing the jewels in hot water.

To dry the gem-set jewels do as the jewellery manufacturers do and place them in a tray of warm boxwood sawdust. This type of sawdust is as fine as dust itself and absorbs all trace of moisture without scratching the surface of the gems. Finally, all traces of the sawdust should be brushed away with a very soft-bristled brush (a complexion brush is ideal for the purpose). Never, in any circumstances, should an attempt be made to clean the interstices of a setting by prodding at them with a pointed implement. It is a sure way of loosening or even damaging the stone and its setting.

In return for the great pleasure the possession of pearls brings to the owner, these gems demand only the simplest of care and attention. Pearls should always be kept from contact with soapy water—and from being sprayed with scent. The surface of a pearl is absorbent and frequent immersion in soapy water may cause discoloration, while contact with scent may cause pitting. For this reason pearls should not be washed, but any film that may cling to them after wear should be removed by wiping them over gently with a soft piece of chamois leather, or fine bran, slightly warmed and placed on the leather, may be rubbed gently over the pearls. As well as keeping pearls apart from other gem-set jewels, they should not be worn in contact with other gems for the same reason—that they may be scratched. And no matter how well they are strung, pearls should be examined by a jeweller from time to time to check up on the stringing and occasionally for professional cleaning. With real pearls of any age which have become discoloured it is possible to have them peeled—clearly a matter for the expert.

Plain gold jewellery will only require to be washed in warm soapy lather, dried on a soft cloth and polished off with a soft chamois leather. Silver jewellery, unless it has become tarnished, may also be cleaned in this way. If it is badly tarnished the simplest and easiest way to restore it is to dip it into a special solution designed for this purpose, leave for a few moments, rinse it with very hot water and then polish off with the specially impregnated cloth which accompanies the silver-dip solution.

Coral, cornelian, lapis lazuli and similar gemstones may be cleaned by a careful washing in warm soapy water, rinsing, drying and finally polishing with a chamois leather. Opals should not be washed, nor should turquoise. Both these gemstones are of a somewhat porous nature and if immersed in water are likely to absorb the moisture and so tend to crack or become discoloured. A lightweight oil should be sparingly applied with a soft cloth to clean these gemstones, finishing off with a soft clean cloth for the final polish. The same cleaning method should be used with mother-of-pearl jewellery.

Marcasite is another 'gemstone' which should not be washed. All that is needed to brighten and clean this type of jewel is to rub it with a soft brush and finish off with a gentle polishing with the chamois leather. For jade the best cleaning medium is black emery or graphite powder—both of which are very soft—applied with a soft cloth and polished off with a chamois leather. Enamelled jewellery should be cleaned by dipping in a mild solution of pure soap-suds and hot water to which a few drops of ammonia have been added. Polish off with a very soft cloth.

Amber, like pearls, needs to be kept apart from other jewellery as its surface is easily scratched. All that is needed to keep it clean and in good condition is careful polishing with a soft cloth. If it has been so neglected that it has become encrusted, a paste made of fine pumice powder mixed with water can be used to clear the surface, with a final polishing with a soft clean cloth.

CHAPTER SEVENTEEN

'Jewel' anniversaries

NOT all wedding anniversaries are commemorated, and surprisingly few people seem to know that there are any other than the generally observed silver, golden and diamond anniversaries. Actually there are eight noteworthy wedding anniversaries featuring jewels and precious metals. These are:

25 years *Silver*
30 years *Pearl*
35 years *Jade or coral*
40 years *Ruby*
45 years *Sapphire*
50 years *Gold*
55 years *Emerald*
60 years *Diamond*

Customarily gifts in the jewel or precious metal appropriate to the anniversary are given by relations and friends of the married couple. The nature and value of such gifts vary, of course, but it is a curious fact that the most generally liked jewel—the diamond—is left until the recipients are well into later life and are hardly likely to be as thrilled as younger married couples would be. Perhaps because of this it is growing more and more the custom to give diamonds as anniversary wedding presents at a much earlier stage—from the first one onwards. Many famous family heirlooms represent such gifts so that the pleasure their original bestowal gave the recipients is shared by succeeding generations.

Index

Named stones are indexed under type of stone; e.g. 'Koh-i-Noor' can be found under 'Diamonds, famous'

ALBERT, Prince Consort, 100
Alexandra, Queen, 59, 75, 86, 97
Alfred, King, 55, 106, 107
Amber, location and qualities, 32–3
Amazonite, 39
Amethysts, 33
  as birthstone, 115
Ampulla, the, 107
Andrew of Greece, Princess, 94
Anniversary jewels, 148
Anointing Spoon, the, 107
Aquamarines, location and qualities, 33–4
  as birthstone, 115–16
Aquarius, sign of, 115
Aries, sign of, 115–16
Australia, precious stone production, 18, 19, 20, 31, 35, 36

BAHREIN, Sheik of, 98
Beryls, 34
'Big Hole', the, 12
Birthstones, 114–20
Black Prince, the, 106, 107–8
Blood, Captain, 108
Boniface IV, Pope, 43
Botha, General, 96
Bracelets, Egyptian, 47
  Greek, 47
  Etruscan and Roman, 47–8
  Byzantine, 48
  Saxon, 48–9
  medieval, 49
  Renaissance, 49
  French, 50
  19th century, 50–1, 78–91
  modern, 51–2

Brazil, precious stone production, 12, 18, 33, 34, 36, 37
Brooches, ancient, 66–8
  medieval, 68–9
  Scottish, 68–9
  Renaissance, 69
  17th and 18th centuries, 69
  19th century, 69–71, 78–91
  modern, 71–2
Brown, Sir Allen, 100
Burma, precious stone production, 20, 22–3, 25, 35, 36

Cabochon cut, 20, 21, 23, 124–5
Cairngorms, 36, 81
Camden, William, 29
Cameos, 81
Cancer, sign of, 117
Capricorn, sign of, 119
Carat weight, 16
Carbuncles, 35
Ceylon, precious stone production, 20, 22, 26, 33, 34, 35, 37, 40
'Chandelier' ear-rings, 63
Charles I, 25, 63
Châtelaines, 85
Citrine, 34
Cleopatra, 17
Conway River, 29
Coral, 81
Cornelians, 34
Coronation Ring, the, 113
Cramp rings, 44
Cromwell, Oliver, 106–7
Crowns, British, 107, 109–11
Cutting, types of, 124–5
  faceting, 125–6

INDEX

DE BEERS, 12, 93
  the 'Charter', 15–7
Decade rings, 44
Diamonds, history and location, 11–13
  alluvial deposits, 12
  the London market, 13
  cleaving and sawing, 13–15, 16–17
  bruting, 14–15
  faceting, 15
  the De Beers Charter, 15–17
  industrial stones, 17
  as birthstone, 116
Diamonds, famous:
  Akbar Shah, 127–8
  Blue Tavernier, 132
  Cullinan, 14, 96, 109, 112
  Darya-i-Noor, 128
  Dresden Green, 128
  English Dresden, 128–9
  Eugénie, 129
  Eureka, 129–30
  Excelsior, 130
  Florentine, 130–1
  Great Mogul, 131
  Hope, 131–2
  Jonker, 132–3
  Jubilee, 133
  Koh-i-Noor, 111, 133–4
  Nassak, 134
  Niarchus, 135
  Nizam, 135–6
  Orloff, 136–7
  Sancy, 137
  Star of Africa, *see* Cullinan
Dutoitspan, 12

EAR-RINGS, Biblical, 61
  Greek, 61–2
  Roman, 61–2
  medieval, 62
  Renaissance, 62–3
  17th and 18th centuries, 63–4
  19th century, 64, 78–91
  modern, 64–5
Edinburgh, Duke of, 93
Edward the Confessor, 106, 107

Edward VII, 96
Emeralds, history and location, 17–19
  qualities, 19
  faceting, 19–20
  cutting, 20
  as birthstone, 116–7
Emeralds, famous:
  Amritsar statuette, 138
  Devonshire, 18
  Queen Mary's, 138
  Tsars', 138
Elizabeth I, 24, 25, 58, 63, 69, 74, 106, 107
Elizabeth II, jewels of, 28, 76–7, 92–100
Elizabeth, the Queen Mother, jewels of, 19, 100–1
Engagement rings, 43–6
Eugénie, Empress, 17–18

FACETING, 15, 125–6
Ferronnière, the, 74, 80

GARNETS, 34–5
  as birthstone, 115
Gemini, sign of, 116–7
Gemmel rings, 44
George I, 99
George IV, 99
George V, 20, 103
George VI, 94, 101, 104
Gipsy rings, 44–5
Girandole, the, 60, 64
Giuliano, 83, 85
Gould, Jay, 88

HAIR ORNAMENTS, ancient, 73
  medieval, 73–4
  Tudor, 74
  18th century, 74–5
  19th century, 75, 78–91
  modern, 75–7
Henrietta Maria, 25
Henry V, 108

INDEX

Henry VIII, 49, 69
Hatpins, 85–6

INDIA, precious stone production, 11–12, 20, 34
Innocent III, Pope, 22
Irt, River, 29

JAGERSFONTEIN, 12
James I, 106–7
Jet, 35, 80
Jewellery, choice of, 140–3
  care of, 144–7
Josephine, Empress, 50

KIMBERLEY, 12, 96
Keeper rings, 45

LEADHILL GOLD MINES, 98–9
Leo, sign of, 117–18
Libra, sign of, 118–19
Lightning Ridge field, 31, 32, 100
London, diamond market, 13

MADAGASCAR, 20, 36
Margaret, Princess, jewels of, 101–5
Margaret, Queen of Scotland, 24
Medici, Catherine de, 25
Mary, Queen (1911–53), 19, 93ff
Mary Stuart, 25, 49
Metropolitan Opera House, 88–9
Mexico, 26, 31–2
Mills, Darius O., 88
Moonstones, 35
  as birthstone, 117
Mourning jewellery, 80, 82
Mozo mines, 18

NAPOLEON III, 17
Necklaces, Egyptian, 53–4
  Greek, 54
  Roman, 54–5

Merovingian, 55
Saxon, 55
medieval, 55
Tudor, 56–7
17th and 18th centuries, 57
19th century, 57–9, 78–91
modern, 57–60

ODONTOLITE, 39
Opals, colour and location, 30–2
  cutting and qualities, 32
  as birthstone, 119
Opals, famous:
  Andamooka, 97
  Roebling, 31
Orbs, the, 112

PAPAL RING, the, 43
Pearls, history, 24–5
  supply, 25
  colour and quality, 26
  markets and grading, 26–7
  cultured, 27
  shape, 27–8
  freshwater, 28–9
  seed, 80, 81
  as birthstone, 117
Pearls, famous, Hanoverian, 138–9
  Marie Antoinette's, 138
  Paragon, 139
Peridots, 35
  as birthstone, 118
Phillips, Robert, 81, 83
Pinchbeck, 82
Pisces, sign of, 115
Pompadour, Madame de, 57
Premier mines, 12

RALEIGH, Sir Walter, 61
Richard III, 108
Rings, as talismans, 41, 44
  Egyptian, 42
  Roman, 42–3
  Celtish, 43
  ecclesiastical, 43

INDEX

Rings, as talismans (*contd.*)
  betrothal, 44–6, 90–1
  modern, 45–6
  coronation, 113
  setting, 124
Rockefeller, William, 88
Rubies, location and colour, 22–3
  synthetic stones, 23
  cutting, 23
  setting, 23–4
  value, 24
  as birthstone, 117–18
Rubies, famous:
  the Black Prince's, 107–8
  the Duke of Marlborough's, 138
  the King of Ceylon's, 137–8
Russia, precious stone production, 18, 33, 34, 36, 37

SAGGITARIUS, sign of, 119
Sapphires, location and colour, 20–1
  structure, 21
  cutting, 21–2
  carving, 22
  as birthstone, 118–19
Sapphires, famous:
  Golden Rose, 22
  St Edward's, 108–9
  Stuart, 109
Sceptres, the British, 112–13
Scorpio, sign of, 119
Settings, box, 121, 124
  invisible, 121–2
  spring, 122–3
  convertible, 123
  flexible, 123
  calibre, 123
  pavé, 123–4
  ring, 124
Shakespeare, William, 61
Shieffelin, Mrs W. H., 89
Siam, 20, 40
'Sights', diamond, 13
'Slave bangle', 51–2

Smuts, General, 96
South Africa, precious stone production, 12, 18–19, 34, 35
Sporting jewellery, 86
Step cutting, 20, 21, 23
Sumptuary Laws, 55
Swords of State, the, 113

TAURUS, sign of, 116
Theodora, Empress, 48
Tiaras, *see* Hair Ornaments
Tiberius, Emperor, 42
Tiffany, 87–91
Topaz, 35–6
  as birthstone, 119
Tourmalines, 36–7
Turquoise, history and location, 37–9
  colour, 37, 38
  qualities, 39–40
  as birthstone, 119–20

URUGUAY, 35
U.S.A., precious stone production, 20, 31, 34, 36, 37, 38
  19th-century jewellery, 87–91

VANDERBILT, Mrs Cornelius, 89
Vanderbilt, William, 88
Venezuela, 26
Victoria, Queen, 25, 28, 64
Virgo, sign of, 118

WATCHES, fob, 91
Wedding rings, 43–6, 90–1
West Indies, 26
Whitby, 35
Williamson, Dr J. N., 95, 102
Wynn, Sir Richard, 29

ZIRCONS, 40
Zodiac, signs of, 114–20